# The Education Formula

# THE EDUCATION FORMULA

## Maximizing the Village

**Berwick Augustin**

EVOKE180 PUBLISHING | LAUDERHILL, FL

Berwick Augustin/Evoke180 Publishing
Lauderhill, FL
www.evoke180.com

Printed in the United States of America

The Education Formula: Maximizing the Village/Berwick Augustin
ISBN 979-8-9884724-0-7 Paperback

*To the tireless advocates, the champions of change, and
the guardians of possibility, whose unwavering dedication
illuminates the path of education. This book is dedicated to you
for your service to give humanity access to the most powerful
civil right everyone deserves to have.*

# ACKNOWLEDGEMENTS

In the journey of creating this book, I have been fortunate to stand on the shoulders of giants, guided by the unwavering support, wisdom, and inspiration of countless individuals. It is with deep gratitude and heartfelt appreciation that I acknowledge those who have played an instrumental role in bringing this vision to life.

To my beloved wife, Gretchen and cherished children, Nyah, Ayana, and Prince, you are the unwavering pillars of love and strength that have fortified my journey in completing this book project. Being your servant leader has been my guiding light through the countless late nights and daunting challenges. Your belief in me when doubt crept in, your smiles that lit up the darkest corners of my writing process, and the warmth of your presence that turned solitude into solace, all played an integral role in bringing this endeavor to fruition. This book stands not just as a culmination of my efforts, but as a tribute to the love, inspiration, and resilience that each of you has infused into every moment of our family's journey. With heartfelt gratitude, I dedicate this work to you, my beloved family, for being the heartbeat of my creativity and the soul of my accomplishment.

To my parents, Jacques and Sainte Rose, for your commitment to faith, family, and education. Those three strands have bound my core values.

To the parents, the first and forever champions of education, whose love and dedication form the bedrock upon which our learners' dreams are built. Your tireless efforts, sacrifices, and reckless belief in the power of education have been the driving force behind this book.

To the principals and leadership teams, the visionaries who navigate the complexities of education with integrity and grace. Your commitment to creating thriving educational ecosystems and empowering your teams has inspired me profoundly, especially the leaders I've had the honor of working with.

To the teachers, the true heroes in the classrooms, who ignite the flames of curiosity and illuminate the paths of learning for our students. Your passion, expertise, and unyielding dedication to nurturing the minds and hearts of our learners have shaped the very fabric of society and this book.

To the community leaders, the bridge builders who bring education and society together, fostering collaboration and collective progress. Your tireless advocacy, partnership, and commitment to equitable educational opportunities have been a beacon of hope and change.

To the students, the vibrant souls who remind us daily of the profound purpose of education. Your resilience, curiosity, and boundless potential have infused this book with the true essence of why we embark on this educational journey.

To the researchers, scholars, and experts who have dedicated their lives to the study and advancement of education, your insights and wisdom have enriched this book and broadened our understanding of the roles and responsibilities of education stakeholders.

To my friends, colleagues, and mentors who have provided guidance, encouragement, and invaluable feedback throughout this journey, your support has been a source of strength and inspiration.

To my publishing team at Evoke180 and all the dedicated professionals who have contributed their expertise and passion to make this book a reality, your commitment to excellence and attention to detail have shaped its final form.

From the bottom of my heart, I thank all of you!

# TABLE OF CONTENTS

# INTRODUCTION

I n the heart of every child lies the flame of curiosity, the spark of potential, and the yearning to learn. Education has the power to ignite that flame, nurture it, and guide it towards illuminating paths of knowledge and opportunity. Yet, as I look upon the education landscape in America, I see a dismal crisis, where the promises of a brighter future for our children are being eclipsed by staggering challenges and systemic shortcomings.

It is with an unwavering determination that I pen this book, *The Education Formula—Maximizing the Village*, fueled by a deep-rooted belief that education is the cornerstone of progress, equality, and human flourishing. I write not as an armchair critic, but as a concerned citizen who has witnessed firsthand the consequences of an ailing education system. I write because I refuse to let our children's dreams be compromised, their potential limited, or their futures dictated by circumstances beyond their control.

The education crisis in America is multifaceted, complex, and far-reaching. It transcends the boundaries of classrooms, school districts, and states, leaving no child unaffected. It is a crisis that perpetuates inequality, societal divisions, and missed opportunities for growth and innovation. It is a crisis that demands urgent attention, relentless advocacy, and transformative action.

Through the pages of this book, I aim to shed light on the pressing issues plaguing our education system, to expose the inequities that hinder progress, and to offer practical solutions and guiding principles that can steer us towards a better future. I write not to assign blame or point fingers, but to ignite a collective sense of responsibility, to rally stakeholders from all walks of life, and to foster a nationwide conversation that compels us to take action.

Within these chapters, we will delve into the challenges faced by students, parents, educators, policymakers, and communities alike. We will confront issues of access and opportunity, equity and inclusivity, curriculum and teaching methodologies, and the critical role of technology in preparing our children for an ever-evolving world. We will examine the importance of fostering critical thinking, creativity, and social–emotional skills that go beyond standardized tests.

But this book is not just about highlighting problems; it is about offering tangible solutions and a road map for change. It is about empowering parents to become advocates for their children's education, inspiring policymakers to enact bold reforms, urging educators to embrace innovative pedagogies, and mobilizing communities to create supportive environments for learning.

Together, we have the power to rekindle the flame of education in America and beyond. We can reshape the narrative, rebuild the foundations, and create an education system that nurtures the unique talents and aspirations of every child, regardless of their zip code or background. This book is a call to action, an impassioned plea to reclaim the promise of education for the sake of our children and the future they deserve.

As we embark on this journey, let us be guided by the unwavering belief that education is not a privilege, but a fundamental right. Let us stand united, driven by compassion and determination, fueled by the belief that the potential within each child is boundless. Let us work together to illuminate the path towards a brighter, more equitable future for every child. Brace yourself for a literary formula:

### Respect + Accountability = Growth

This formula is uniquely relevant to education's various stakeholders, and challenges them to unlock the destinies and limitless potential they possess to shape the hearts and minds of generations to come.

## WHAT THIS BOOK IS

This book is a comprehensive exploration of the education crisis in America, offering an in-depth analysis of the challenges and short-comings that hinder our educational system. It provides a platform for meaningful discussions and reflections on the pressing issues that impact students, parents, educators, policymakers, and communities across the nation. It delves into the complexities of access, equity, curriculum, teaching methodologies, and the integration of technology, providing evidence-based insights and practical solutions to drive positive change.

Through research, case studies, and personal anecdotes, this book presents a compelling argument for the urgent need to transform education in America. It aims to inspire readers to become agents of change and advocates for educational equity, empowering them with knowledge, resources, and a road map for action. The book goes beyond mere critique, offering a holistic perspective on the challenges and opportunities that lie ahead, inviting readers to be part of a collaborative effort to reshape the future of education.

## WHAT THIS BOOK IS NOT

This book is not a quick-fix manual with all-encompassing solutions that claim to single-handedly solve the complex education crisis. It acknowledges the multifaceted nature of the challenges we face and recognizes that meaningful change requires a collective effort from all stakeholders. It is not a finger-pointing exercise that assigns blame, but rather a call to action that encourages empathy, collaboration, and shared responsibility.

While this book provides insights and recommendations, it does not claim to have all the answers. It recognizes that every community, district, and state has unique circumstances, and that tailored approaches are necessary to address their specific needs. It does not dismiss the achievements and dedication of educators, but rather seeks to support and amplify their voices in the quest for educational improvement.

Furthermore, this book is not a pessimistic portrayal of the education system, but rather an optimistic exploration of its potential. It highlights success stories, innovative initiatives, and promising practices that exist across the country, demonstrating that positive change is indeed possible. It seeks to inspire readers to believe in the transformative power of education and to become active participants in shaping a future where every child can thrive.

In essence, this book is a call to action, a catalyst for change, and a guide for those who seek to make a difference in the lives of our children. It invites readers to join a national conversation, to challenge the status quo, and to work towards an education system that upholds respect, inclusivity, and growth for all.

# PARENTS

If you don't educate your children at home, the world will gladly destroy their future for you.

# Primary Educators

From conception to birth, you guide with care.
Parents, the primary educators, are always there
To teach us to crawl, walk, and run
To utter our first words with lots of fun.
You, teach us values, right from wrong
To be respectful, compassionate, and strong,
Through the vein of your patience and love we learn
The flow of responsibility, curiosity, and to discern.
Through joy, tears, laughter, and pain
A parent's love remains the same.
Adolescent actions aren't always worthy of praise
Parents of prodigal children help them find their ways.
Train us to triumph over this harsh world from birth
To know our identity, purpose, and endless worth.
On the bricks of your foundation, we stand
Until your guidance leads us to the promised land.

# 1 | EDUCATION STARTS AT HOME

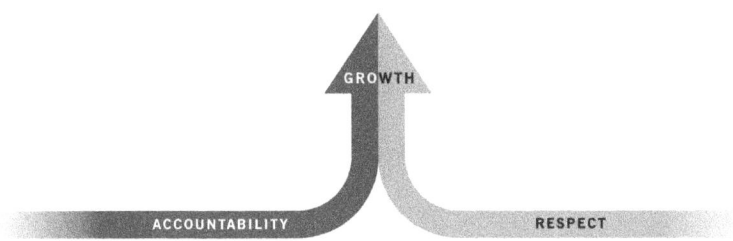

## Respect + Accountability = Growth

Raising little humans is a battlefield like no other. Yes, children are a blessing! The process of pregnancy to giving birth is exhilarating, and the reality of watching a reproduced part of you walk on this earth is transforming. However, once your precious little infant comes out of the womb and begins to cry, a litany of responsibilities begins. Education is at the core of it all. Many of us solicit advice from parenting classes, family, friends, or any other sources that seem to be knowledgeable.

Despite the assistance, we find out that there is no foolproof manual to parenting. The reality of it is if you don't educate your children at home, the world will gladly destroy their future for you. As a parent of three, I've come to realize that there is no easy button when it comes to raising children, and the determining factor of whether or not your babies succeed in life depends on the foundation you set at home.

As guardians, we play a critical role in our children's development, and being the first educator can have a significant impact on their success later in life. Research has shown that children who receive a solid educational foundation at home tend to do better in school, have higher self-esteem, and are more likely to achieve their goals.

Before we get into the nuts and bolts of parenting, I believe it's critical to emphasize the importance of practicing self-care. It has consistently been proven that parents need to prioritize self-care for their overall well-being and their ability to effectively fulfill their parenting responsibilities. Numerous studies have shown that parental self-care positively influences parental mental health, reduces stress levels, and improves overall life satisfaction. Engaging in self-care activities has been associated with lower levels of parental burnout and decreased symptoms of anxiety and depression.

Additionally, research suggests that when parents prioritize self-care, they experience improved emotional regulation, leading to more positive parent–child interactions and enhanced parenting efficacy. Furthermore, practicing self-care serves as a role model for children, teaching them the value of self-care and healthy coping strategies. Whether it's occasionally treating oneself, setting boundaries, prioritizing sleep and physical health, or engaging in activities you enjoy, taking care of yourself is essential. By engaging in self-care, parents are better equipped to meet the demands of parenting, experience greater satisfaction in their roles, and cultivate a nurturing and supportive environment for their children's development.

The education you provide is golden, goes beyond academics, and has many layers to it. A study by the Harvard Family Research Project found that "Family involvement in education can be a more powerful force in a child's academic success than even school itself." This involvement includes not only academic support but also emotional support, such as a positive home environment and fostering a sense of belonging and motivation. In doing so, healthy relationships will be built, and respect will be at the core of them. It is arguably the most important layer and character trait you can teach your children. Respect builds bridges, and the absence of it creates wars. It is a fundamental value human beings need to function properly in every aspect of life.

A highly effective classroom is one that functions with routines and systems to maximize children's intellectual, social, and emotional growth. The most skilled educator who is able to master the aforementioned traits, will not be efficient if students are not equipped with the foundational skills of respect and following directions. As a parent, you play a major role in instilling those characteristics.

Newborns learn routines at a very early age. When they cry, their guardians feed and soothe them. Once that happens, the wailing typically ceases. In essence, parents are a child's first regulator. Early on, guardians are in powerful positions to assist their children with regulating their emotions. This is vital for following instructions, because the infants begin to understand how to respond to authority. From that point, they learn proper manners and character traits from the adults they are surrounded by. Those grown-ups are the village that represent the paintbrush that will either paint a child into a masterpiece or a mess.

As a former educator and school administrator for over two decades, I guarantee that if teachers have classrooms full of students who respect authority and follow instructions, they will have a greater probability of being highly effective educators. In essence, for your child to have access to a better education, a large part of it will be based on the groundwork you lay at home years before your child enters a classroom.

## The Impact of Responsibility

Respect and responsibility are first cousins. They're related and interconnected on many levels. One of the easiest ways parents can help their children learn responsibility is by giving them household chores. It will assist with understanding the value of hard work, which is a crucial skill in the classroom. According to the Center for Parenting Education, children who do have a set of chores have higher self-esteem, are more responsible, and are better able to deal with frustration and delayed gratification, all of which contribute to greater success in school.

Again, I'd like to reiterate that, as parents, you are your child's most important educator and role model. It is your responsibility to set the tone about the importance and the attitude associated with it. My wife and I started assigning tasks to our children at the tender age of three in progressive stages. The tasks weren't based on size, but rather the responsibility as a contributor to the family. More importantly, we modeled completion of household chores without a grudge. As they grew and mastered the initial assignments, the difficulty increased. This helped them do their best and have a sense of pride about their work. Such skill sets are transferable in the classroom and in everyday life. Eventually, we attached an allowance to their chores to help teach financial literacy, but it was clear that completing the chore had to be done to determine if they got paid or not.

On the contrary, it's vitally important for parents to be mindful not to give the kids more responsibility than they can handle because the process will backfire on them. They will perceive responsibility as punishment. For instance, I've had students in the classroom who were overburdened with chores and the task of taking care of younger siblings. Not only did this impact their abilities to manage time, but they also suffered academically. A healthy balance and open communication are critical for optimal results when assigning chores to children. Check in with them to give them voice in the process by inquiring about how they feel in reference to their responsibilities. It's a great way to get buy-in and cooperation to ensure that the job is done well.

Research by Marty Rossman indicates that, "The best predictor of young adults' success in their mid-twenties was that they participated in household tasks when they were three or four." Ultimately, when parents empower their children with responsibility through chores, they are equipping the youth with a sense of ownership, time management, discipline, and the ability to function independently in the home, school, and the outside world.

Additionally, respect can manifest by the way scholars value adults and authority. Your little ones are watching every move you make and every word you say. If they constantly see you break rules by running red lights and doing the opposite of what you tell them to do, you're teaching them how to be defiant and defy authority. If your style of communication is disrespectful and combative, they will mimic the same mannerism with everyone they encounter, including adults. If you converse with them with foul language and slang, they will regurgitate the same rhetoric verbally and in writing. As a former writing teacher, I used to tell parents all the time that students write the way they speak. One simple and effective way guardians can assist their child's writing abilities is by speaking to them in complete and appropriate sentences.

The message of honoring and respecting adults can be taught in many different ways. Growing up in a Haitian household, respect was nonnegotiable. If a visiting adult entered our home, the children were expected to greet the grown-up with a kiss on the cheek. The same rule applied if our family visited someone else's home. Failure to do so resulted in serious consequences.

In terms of school, I remember being in school in Haiti, and whenever the teacher or any adult walked in the room, everyone in the class had to stand until the adult, whether it was the principal or the janitor, directed the class to sit down. When I migrated to Miami at the age of ten, I quickly realized that those simple and powerful gestures were nonexistent at the school I was attending.

That was one of many culture shocks I had to adjust to. In 2012, I went to Kenya, Africa, on a mission trip for a teacher exchange support program. At the time, I was a veteran teacher in the United States for about six years. I shadowed a Kenyan educator who taught a classroom of about fifty students. The minute I walked into the room, all the scholars immediately stood up and remained standing. For a split second, I was confused as to why they got up, but I quickly had a flashback and recalled my childhood custom in Haiti. The African teacher smiled and reminded me that they won't sit down until I directed them to. Nostalgia took my emotions hostage and reminded me of how much educators should be respected and valued. I politely asked the scholars to have a seat.

I spent the entire day with that teacher, interacting with different classes. Despite the large class size, we did not have any behavior issues. Imagine the same scenario with fifty students in an American classroom—the result will look a lot different.

When I returned to Miami, I incorporated the same system in my classroom. Initially, there was some pushback by the students because I was the only teacher in the entire school who was implementing the

11

greeting. Shortly after, it became the norm for my scholars. Needless to say, respect, classroom management, and the culture in my space evolved to a higher level.

Trust me, I had my share of students who made the transition difficult, but they were the minority. They eventually learned how to get in line the hard way. My job would've been easier if these young people had guardians who enforced respect as a core value in their homes. Ultimately, my students' academic achievements increased tremendously that school year, because distractions were replaced by bell-to-bell instructions. Lastly, the substitute teachers for my class didn't have a lot of issues because the level of respect was established and understood. The students showed up for me whether I was in the classroom or not. Respect for every adult was standard, they didn't want to disappoint me, and they also knew that there would be consequences if I received bad reports.

Parents and guardians, this is the type of powerful impact you should have on your kids. In doing so, you will create a fruitful experience for everyone who partners with you to help you educate your children.

## The Humanity of Compassion

Another important component of respect that children need to learn at home is compassion, because it encourages kindness, patience, understanding, and fosters healthy tolerance of others. It can look and feel different at various settings and circumstances. Teaching kids how to say *please* and *thank you* will help them go a long way in life. Kind words are vitamins that are vital for social growth. These are a few necessary tools for daily functioning in the classroom and beyond.

One of the most powerful ways to teach children compassion and respect is to have them volunteer in the community. Imagine if the youth were required to serve the elderly in their formative years. They would have a better appreciation for life and the privilege of acquiring wisdom from elders. Such a simple, yet powerful task would teach young people the respect for adults, themselves, and their peers. They would learn how to treat others the way that they want to be treated. Consequently, it can help curtail the high rate of bullying, fights, and suicide. Research confirms that compassion has a ripple effect in a child's education and general life. A kind scholar produces positive peer interaction, improved behavior, healthy school climate, and higher academic achievement (Greater Good Science Center)

It is important to mention children who are in the foster care system. Unfortunately, many families are broken and dysfunctional. Many studies estimate that roughly 80 percent of children have been exposed to trauma, which negatively impacts brain development and learning. A child who lives in fear, self-preservation, and survival mode cannot focus on schooling. If you are an individual who is overseeing children in this capacity, my plea is for you to be informed, involved, and open. It requires a significant amount of patience and training to successfully create a safe haven at home and school for these babies. Be honest, if you don't have the capacity, please remove yourself from the equation instead of adding more tension to the strained situation. There are organizations that provide effective training, tips, counseling services, support groups, and tools that will set you up for success.

You can take some critical steps to overcome the challenges of being a guardian. First, you have to take care of yourself. You are no good to a child, or the world for that matter, if you are not in a healthy place. Be sure to get enough sleep, eat well, and make time for self-care activities and hobbies. Second, you have to be consistent. Children thrive on routine and consistency. Do your best to establish a daily routine for meals, bedtime, and other activities, and stick to it as much as possible. Third, setting boundaries is essential. Children need to know the difference between acceptable and unacceptable behaviors. Be clear and consistent about your expectations and consequences for misbehavior. At the same time, it's important to balance things out by practicing positive discipline that focuses on teaching children appropriate behavior rather than punishing them. This includes positive reinforcement, such praise and rewards.

Lastly, be open to learning. Parenting is a continual learning process. Every day, I'm realizing the more I learn, the more I need to learn. I'm open to ideas and approaches that are aligned with my values and belief system. Your journey will be unique and tailored to you and your family. The bottom line is for you to position yourself to grow consistently.

Building character traits will only work once you've built a level of trust with a child. Moreover, it will take a village approach to nurse these scholars back to healthy conditions. The more adults they have as champions pouring into them, the better the results will be. However, if inconsistency sets in, everyone's job will be more difficult. At that point, the suffering will trickle down to the child, guardian, community, society, and ultimately our world. It is a must that you engage in advocating for the child, and have clear and constant communication with teachers, counselors, and other pertinent stakeholders.

## CHAPTER TAKEAWAYS

By engaging in self-care, parents are better equipped to meet the demands of parenting, experience greater satisfaction in their roles, and cultivate a nurturing and supportive environment for their children's development.

- If you don't educate your children at home, the world will gladly destroy their future for you.
- Respect builds bridges, and the absence of it creates wars. It is a fundamental value that human beings need to function properly in every aspect of life.
- When parents empower their children with responsibility through chores, they are equipping the youth with a sense of ownership, time management, discipline, and the ability to function independently.

## PROBE AND TRANSFORM

How does your engagement as a parent in your child's education foster a sense of connection, support, and attitude towards learning?

- How do you encourage your children to explore new ideas, ask questions, and seek knowledge?
- How do you collaborate with teachers and educators to support your child's learning and academic success?
- How do you incorporate learning opportunities into everyday routines and activities at home?

# Speak Up

In the halls of learning,

Young minds roam

There's a dire need for advocates

To guarantee no child is left alone.

Parents, you hold the key

To unlock your child's potential.

Access and support are significant

Your constant engagement is essential.

In a cruel and unforgiving world,

Your watchful eye will give your child a chance

To see justice and an equitable education

Or else they'll perish and won't advance.

Without your voice to speak up,

They'll suffer in silence and won't be heard.

With every fiber of your being

Advocate with every breath and every word.

# 2 | ADVOCATING

## *Respect* + Accountability = **Growth**

When parents don't speak up and get involved in their child's education, they leave the scholar exposed and unprotected. Because education starts at home, guardians are the front line of defense for children. Prior to students starting school, parents are the best advocates because they've spent the most time with them and understand their strengths and weaknesses. Leveraging that information is crucial for keeping scholars honest about the expectations you have for them. Although there are various ways you can be involved in your child's education, I'll focus on three: teacher support, knowing your rights, and telling your story.

## Teacher Support

Partnering with your child's school, specifically the classroom teachers, will create a level of accountability for all stakeholders. The scholar's behavior and effort tend to be more focused if they know the connection exists, and happens often. The educator will be challenged to do right by the child on every level, knowing there's a check and balance system with guardians. As parents, the partnership will give you the peace of mind of knowing you're getting valuable insight to help you make informed decisions about your child's educational future. Again, I'd like to reiterate that, as the primary educator, your kid's teachers are your strongest allies.

In reality, for the parents who don't get involved in their children's education because they don't feel comfortable navigating the school systems, please understand that being silent and idle is the worst solution you can come up with. Being uncomfortable signals you about an opportunity for growth. Besides, as a parent, I can't imagine too many things, if any, more important to me than supporting my child to thrive in school and beyond.

In addition to accountability at home, guardians nowadays have a variety of ways to communicate with educators and the school staff. They can ask questions via phone, text, email, virtual conference, group chats, social media platforms, and different means of communication. If language is a barrier, schools are required to provide you with equitable access in your native language. School districts should also have parent advocates designated to help you understand your rights and how to maximize the free services you're entitled to. At the end of the day, you have to ask!

## Know Your Rights

Do you know that there are statutes and laws in place specifically written for parents regarding students' records, rights, and educational provisions? As much as they're powerful, and have the ability to give you access, they're useless if you don't utilize them.

I know what you're thinking, "I don't have the time and capacity to read some legal paperwork!" I get it. The good news is you're not alone, and you have help! There are tons of nonprofit organizations and faith-based congregations on just about every corner in every major city and all over the internet. Most, if not all, provide free resources to assist with any services you may need.

Leaders and elected officials in your community are valuable resources that parents should be partnering with. Do not be afraid to lean on the people in your village. Your local mayors, commissioners, and other government officials are tasked with the holistic development of the communities they govern. During election time, they are not ashamed nor afraid to knock on your doors, come to your churches, and flood your phones and street corners with promotional materials to ask for your votes and donations for their electoral campaigns.

Likewise, you should not be timid about inquiring about assistance when it comes to your family's needs. Not to mention it is your tax dollars that fund their salaries, the educational system, and any other public works. If you are a spiritual person, engage your faith-based organization in the conversation, because they, too, have access to help you advocate beyond your individual capacity.

Lastly, every public school has a Parent Teacher Association (PTA) that is made up of dedicated parents and school staff who meet at least once a month to plan how to better serve the school and scholars with necessary resources. A study published in the *Journal of Educational Research* found that schools with active PTAs had higher levels of parent involvement and greater student achievement than schools without active PTAs. The study suggests that PTAs can provide a forum for parents to connect with each other and with teachers, and can help support education in the community (Gonzalez-DeHass & Willems 2003).

I spent over two decades working in South Florida's urban schools that are similar to Miami's Little Haiti neighborhood, where I grew up. It has been disheartening to see the low engagement and lack of parent attendance in PTA meetings. Although our communities need support, the people who are in positions to provide the resources will not allocate them if you don't speak up. Their irrational rationale is, if you don't say anything, you must not be in need. I'm not oblivious to the social economic obstacles that exist within my community. Working multiple jobs, lack of transportation, and other challenges are real, but you have to find a way to get involved. Trust me, the majority of schools should be flexible to work with you. Besides, they are all mandated by law to do so. While many schools may be eager to get you on board because they understand the impact of your involvement, others may not be as welcoming. Do not allow that to discourage you. You have to be relentless in making sure you stand in the gap for the children, because their future depends on it.

If for some reason you're dealing with a school that's not cooperative, be sure to do your due diligence by documenting your efforts-save text messages, emails, and phone call attempts you've made that have gone by the wayside. From that point, move on to the next step by contacting the school's district office via phone or letter. Engage other guardians in your neighborhood who may be experiencing the same thing. There is power when you move with a group of like-minded people. Again, this is where your local officials and faith-based organizations can provide assistance, by coming alongside you to stand up for educational equity.

## Tell Your Story

Everyone has a story that matters and needs to be heard. Neuroscience research confirms that storytelling is a powerful way to build empathy and can serve as a catalyst for change and problem-solving. Parents, imagine your narrative navigating through a school to help wash away behavioral problems. Better yet, it can be at the center of professional development for teachers and practitioners to strengthen their practices as professionals. Yes, your story has the capacity to do that!

Before we focus outwards, let's zoom inwards—the impact of your story has to travel from the inside out. As parents, I know you want your children to have a good education. They need to know your "why." After I graduated high school, I remember getting ready to go away to college. Days before my departure, my mom pulled me to the side. We sat on the porch. She looked me in the eyes with tears rolling down her cheeks and asked me to promise to come back home with a degree. She went on to tell me about the sacrifices she and my dad made for me and my siblings to have access to opportunities they had only dreamed of.

Needless to say, I did not see that story coming, but it kept me motivated on many occasions when I felt like giving up during my collegiate career.

During my tenure as teacher and administrator, I asked a plethora of guardians if they ever told their children their stories. More than 90 percent of them said no. Caregivers, I know you care about your scholars, but I need you to understand that there's power in the bumps of the road you've traveled. It's information you don't have to research or study. It's embedded in your psyche. It's in your heart because it's part of who you are. It's also a major part of your children's identity, culture, and self-worth. Once you release that vital information into their minds, it will unleash intrinsic motivation that will assist them in the classroom and beyond. Of course, be wise in terms of making sure you share age-appropriate content. Ultimately, the learned lessons and high expectations should be at the root of your storytelling.

Once your children know your family's story, their educators should be aware of the destination you envision for your babies. Believe it or not, some teachers really believe disengaged parents don't care about their children's future. While there may be some outliers who fit the mold, I can attest that the vast majority of guardians are genuinely concerned. One of the most powerful ways to dispel this myth is to let the educators know your vision and mission for your kids. I would go as far as writing it down before you share it with them to make sure you articulate it loud and clear. In addition, you can jot down your concerns on a sheet of paper as well to reiterate your expectations. This will help answer a lot of questions, facilitate understanding, and build a strong relationship with the educators in the school. After all, they are your vital helpers. Together, you can develop a plan tailored for the success of your scholar. Later in the book, I will offer some practical ways schools can engage parents with storytelling. Remember, your child will only go as far as the bridge you build for them. Begin to create the trust that will sustain strong accountability with the community that is helping you raise your children.

In addition to your child's school, there are a number of community organizations that can assist you. Libraries and community centers can provide access to books, educational materials, technology, and programs to help you. After-school programs also provide children with learning opportunities and academic support. Best of all, most of them are FREE! Additionally, they provide workshops, parenting classes, and other valuable resources that will help strengthen your plight as a parent.

A study published in the *Journal of Education for Students Placed at Risk* found that parents who had access to community resources such as libraries, community centers, and after-school programs reported higher levels of involvement in their children's education. This study suggests that providing access to resources can help parents become more engaged in their children's learning (Ferguson & Mueller 2017).

As a parent, your involvement as an advocate is critical to ensuring that your children receive a high-quality education and support. Furthermore, your voice is powerful enough to help shape education policy and decisions at the local, state, and national level. You already have a massive number of resources at your disposal. You simply need to engage them. If you don't know how to get involved, please ask. In order to obtain positive outcomes for your children both academically and beyond, you have to be at the center of the accountability formula.

## CHAPTER TAKEAWAYS

When parents don't speak up and get involved in their child's education, they leave the scholar exposed and unprotected.

- Schools with active Parent Teacher Associations (PTAs) have higher levels of parent involvement and greater student achievement than schools without active PTAs.
- You have to be relentless in making sure that you stand in the gap for your children, because their futures depend on it.
- Learned lessons and high expectations should be at the root of your storytelling.

## PROBE AND TRANSFORM

How can you ensure that your child's needs, interests, and strengths are recognized and addressed in the educational setting?

- What obstacles or barriers have you encountered when advocating for your child's education? How are you seeking support?
- How can parents begin to advocate effectively for their children?
- How do you stay informed and up-to-date with your child's academic progress, curriculum, and school policies?

# Active Engagement

A child's education
Requires more than passive participation
It's about accountability being more than a word,
It's actively engaging in a promise and commitment
That transforms dreams into futures that gleam.
Parents grounded in the educational plight
Day in and day out.
Their support is never in doubt
Despite the highs and lows
Children grow when guardians stand up
To systems that are corrupted
With gangrene practices, poli-tricks, and privileges.
Parents partnering with local businesses
Seeking support from the surrounding community
To gain necessary access to fulfill needs to succeed
Guardian gatekeepers, it's your accountability
That determines your child's education and destiny.

# 3 | ACCOUNTABILITY

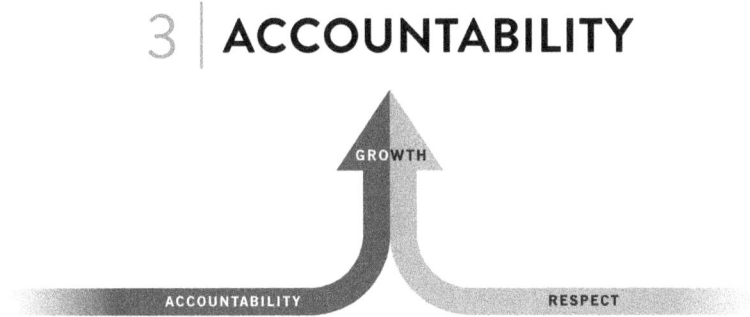

*Respect* **+** Accountability **= Growth**

As a parent, your attitude towards education is paramount for children. After you lay the foundation from the toddler years to primary and secondary school, please understand that your intentional support as a coach and facilitator will continue to be important for the rest of their lives. The way you feel and think about education can be highly contagious in your household. It's up to you whether that virus is beneficial or detrimental.

Accountability is one of the pillars for character. It requires commitment, breeds collaboration, builds capacity, instills value, and provides results. In order for accountability to thrive, it needs to be nurtured with healthy attitudes, boundaries, and relationships. It stands as a beacon, illuminating the path of parental duty and underscoring the significance of active engagement in their children's educational journey. With each delicate step, accountability entrusts parents with the unwavering resolve to provide a sturdy foundation, demanding unwavering attention, and unwrapping the gift of quality time. It urges them to be resolute in the face of challenges, championing their children's progress, and remaining vigilant stewards of their academic pursuits.

I want to reiterate that guardians will always be a child's most important educator. I've been reading to my three bundles of joy since the moment they were conceived in the womb, and I won't ever stop reading to them as their father. Studies have proven that reading to babies in the womb helps with brain development. As they grow, the reading turns into robust conversation that facilitates comprehension and vocabulary.

Every single day is packed with a world of opportunities to help young minds make sense of schooling with real-world connections that bring education to life. The best part about it is when you use your daily activities and interactions as teachable moments. My wife creates fun and simple tasks like baking cakes with our little ones. While they're enjoying the experience of tasting the batter, they're reading recipe instructions, practicing math by measuring ingredients, and understanding science by conversing about what makes the mixed elements rise in the oven. That one task covers many educational disciplines and life skills.

There are times I have them reenact scenes from a book they've read. In doing so, they're developing critical thinking skills, imaginative thinking, inferencing, comprehension, and vocabulary. This is a fun and effective way for them to learn and grow.

As a matter of fact, a review of research on the benefits of imaginative play published in the *American Journal of Play* suggests that reenacting stories can help children develop social emotional skills, including empathy, self-regulation, and conflict resolution (Lillard et al. 2013). Lord knows, the ability to resolve conflicts effectively is a dire need in our world. It behooves you as a parent to be a change agent by empowering your child with such a vital life skill. It doesn't require a degree, certification, or a lot of time from your busy schedule.

If you are one of the parents who feels intimidated by the complexity of your child's schoolwork, I want you to know that it's not a bad idea to allow yourself to be vulnerable during these precious moments. There will be times when you may not know the answer to a problem; it's okay to inform your child that you don't know. You can explore, read, and learn together to send them a message that learning is a lifelong process. Furthermore, it will encourage your child to be resourceful when faced with difficulties and comfortable with asking for help when necessary. Maximize the teachable moments in your daily routines with your children, because they will become the soundtracks, legacy clips, and heritage they pass down to the next generation.

## Healthy Boundaries

Healthy boundaries are necessary for self-care, safety, and respect. Explicitly teaching and modeling limits to their children early and often is vital for parents. They are life skills that are transferable to the classroom and beyond. Because we're living in the information age, technology has become intensely intrusive. Parents have to be just as aggressive to combat the onslaught of distractions bombarding the minds of the youth. Technology should not be used as a pacifier. You have to limit your child's screen time, because it has become an addiction that is responsible for major health issues. It affects eyesight, ability to sleep, mental health, and increases the risk of weight gain. Not to mention the inappropriate content your children are viewing if you're not monitoring what they have access to on their electronic devices. If you don't set boundaries for your kids in the virtual world, you will lose them in real life.

Adolescents who compromise sleep for electronics are more likely to have behavior and attention problems in school, which will contribute to poor academic performance. Research confirms that parents who work on learning activities at home with their children are utilizing the most effective kind of parenting approach. As hard it may seem, you have to find ways for you and your kids to put the electronics away for more meaningful interactions. "Nothing has to take more than five minutes, and yet what you've done is you've conveyed to your child, 'I care about you, I care about what you're learning . . . And isn't this an interesting world?'" says Dorothy Rich, author of the MegaSkills book series, which includes many home learning activities for families.

Parents, you have to be a doer of the advice you give to your children. They will have more respect for you when you model the integrity and characteristics you want to pass down to them. As a child, I didn't fully understand the notion: "I'm not your friend; I'm your parent."

It made so much sense to me, however, when I had firsthand experience of witnessing the damages caused to my scholars by the irresponsible actions of their guardians. I'm talking about elementary school kids smoking marijuana with their parents, the use and abuse of pornography, and a host of destructive behaviors I prefer not to mention.

I'm not here to tell you how to raise your children, but hear me out for a minute. When you send your babies to school, it's a nonverbal communication that lets them know you want them to be equipped with skills to better themselves as adults. However, the minute you engage them in the devastating habits I named, you're not only confusing them by breaking the law, but you also stunt their growth academically, mentally, and emotionally. It's like planting a seed, never watering it, digging it up every other day, but expecting it to flourish.

One of the most heartbreaking scenarios I endured was the negative impact of a father while teaching a group of young third-grade boys. Every Wednesday, I had my students dress up in slacks, a long-sleeve button-down shirt, and a tie. Initially, they resisted the initiative because they were the only ones in the entire school who had to participate. It wasn't the norm. After a while, they bought into it and owned the fact that they were professionally dressed once a week. I had a particular young man who struggled more than the others because I wouldn't allow him to sag his pants. After a while, he eventually got on board.

The minute he felt comfortable with the movement, we hit a brick wall. His dad was released from prison and resisted all the work I'd done. He would come to school to pick up the young man with his pants almost down to his knees. When I approached dad about the situation, his response was, "I told him he has to do the opposite of what I do because I want him to be more successful than I am in life."

While those words may sound endearing, Dad's actions were grossly misaligned with the good intentions he might have had. A massive amount of research proves that fathers play a crucial role in their sons' development and that their involvement and support have lasting effects. It's up to the father to determine whether the effects are positive or negative. Although I communicated consistently with the dad and built a rapport with him throughout the school year, the young man struggled because the standards at home and in school were inconsistent. I've not been in contact with the young man since that school year. I can only hope his father made better parental choices in raising him.

I remember when I was in middle school in Miami, my dad randomly showed up to the school to check on my sister and me. This man would show up with his broken English, vest, shirt, and tie like he was about to preach at church. If you know anything about old-school Haitian parents, they get dressed up to go to the corner store. Most importantly, they do not like to look bad in what they consider to be the "Holy Trinity" of life—Lekòl, Legliz, Lakay, which translates to school, church, and home.

Although I hated the unwanted visits, they kept me in check because he was liable to pop up at any time. God forbid, if he received a phone call from a teacher about me misbehaving, my punishment was unadulterated. Whatever I had to say was irrelevant, because his approach was, if the teacher had to stop what he or she was doing to contact him about my misconduct, that was enough evidence for him to know that I was in the wrong. He didn't care about how it happened or who else was involved. Every single day, he stressed to us that he was doing his best to cross barriers to advocate for us to have a better life than he did. Our job was to go to school, follow instructions, do our work, and not get caught up with anything or anyone around us who could hinder that process. Even though language and culture posed a threat to the parent–teacher partnership, my dad's actions enabled the unity to be aligned because his engagement spoke volumes to the educators at the school. Gone are those parenting days for most of our students. In the same vein, I wholeheartedly applaud the parents, especially the men, who are present and active in educating their children.

Nowadays, some students use their parents to threaten teachers. They are not afraid of phone calls home because they know there are no consequences. Some are compensated with "gifts and rewards" after mishaps or bad grades. Others will say things like, "I'm going to make my mom or dad come to the school to curse you out . . ." or whatever expletive rhetoric they feel compelled to use.

Don't get me wrong. I'm not implying that all teachers are upstanding and righteous, but I do believe that parents play a major role in maintaining the unity of the educational marriage. It starts with accountability and encouraging respectful interactions. You have to make it clear to your child that you've partnered with the educators to enhance his or her educational success. Caretakers who model respect or a high view of educators tend to benefit more. When they do, their children have no choice but to follow their lead.

On the other hand, guardians who do the opposite usually create a combative and ineffective situation for all parties. Studies have proven that healthy parent involvement in school is a strong factor in student accomplishments.

Parents, as you show up for your students, you will teach them how to advocate for themselves. One of the most powerful movements benefiting education today is student-led parent–teacher conferences. Instead of scholars sitting in these traditional meetings as bystanders or absent altogether, they become the center of attention by leading the sessions. They're able to show the work they've done in class and articulate their academic progress or lack thereof. I strongly encourage you to contact your child's school and request that teachers work with him or her on how to facilitate such a conference. According to studies, researchers recommend flipping the format because it guarantees student engagement, responsibility for their learning, and student voice.

From the time I was four to ten years old, I lived in Haiti with my aunt and a slew of cousins. Although her level of education wasn't high, she made sure she kept every child in the house in line academically. Whenever we came home from school, she would simply ask us to explain what we learned in every subject that day. She would listen intently to recognize if we paid attention and were able to articulate the learned lessons. She would always say, "If you can explain it, then I know you learned something for the day." God forbid if one of us lied or tried to repeat something from the previous day; a good ol' country butt "whooping" went into full effect!

This was before the age of technology, emails, text messages, virtual meetings, etc. The message was clear: education was nonnegotiable, and accountability was consistent. Her communication with the school was very simple. If we were not on task and on point, the professors were granted the right to discipline us however they saw fit before they called home. They were empowered with the notion that they were the parents away from home.

The level of trust and respect for educators was huge in my beloved country, Haiti. A nation's culture towards education plays a major role in its success on every level. Imagine the culture shock of my parents and their counterparts who migrated from Haiti to America, only to find out they had to adjust to a myriad of things, including the language, systems, and procedures. On one hand, they have a strong desire to be the school's accountability partners. On the other hand, they lack the ability to access information, resources, and services to do the latter.

Despite limited assistance, guidance, and discrimination, I'm blessed and fortunate that my parents were able to overcome the barriers. This was possible because they didn't waver when it came to their core values and eventually connected with a small village of people who helped us along the way. At the end of the day, it was their relentless approach to education that propelled our family to succeed.

I don't know how else to stress the truth about education starting at home. If you don't remember anything else from this book, please tattoo that in your brain. Parents give birth to little humans and inherit the hefty task to raise them into productive citizens. It starts with respect and making sure your children understand what it looks like, feels like, and sounds like. As they grow, engage them in responsible family functions like preparing the shopping list. Teach them how to think critically and empower them with financial literacy, so they can be confident as independent learners who make informed decisions as they grow. This will facilitate the gradual release of owning their education and future.

Fathers, you are the head of the home who brings structure and stability. Mothers, you help support Dad with irreplaceable nurture and child-rearing. With unified discipline, you cement the evidence to prove that family is the cornerstone of the community, the backbone of schools, and the educational mecca society needs to thrive. If you are a single parent, I applaud you for carrying the heavy weight on your own. If possible, do your best to leverage your family and community to lighten the load.

I remember sitting at a parent–teacher conference with a mother and her son. She was furious and frustrated about having to come to the school to address her child's behavior and academic apathy. She blamed me, the school, and negative peer influences. Throughout her discourse, the mom did not associate responsibility to herself or her child.

I calmly looked into her eyes and uttered, "I'm not responsible for your child's education. You are the teacher. I'm here to help you." With a confused expression, she became more agitated by my response. I went on to explain to her that, "I have her child for a season, but she has him for a lifetime."

By the end of the conference, I saw the lightbulbs turning on in her brain as she asked problem-solving questions that facilitated a healthier meeting. In reality, after those ten months in the fifth grade, I've never laid eyes on that young man again. Today, I can only hope that the mom took my advice to heart and owned her child's education instead of putting it on everyone else.

An educator's job is to come alongside parents to help them educate their children. In order for that assistance to effectively take place, the scholars have to come to school with foundational skills that can only be learned at home. I had a colleague who taught kindergarten break it down this way (paraphrased): "From birth to five years old, parents are with their children one thousand eight hundred and twenty-five days. Some of the babies come to me not knowing their alphabets, even worse their names. Somehow, I'm expected to teach them the alphabets, how to count, colors, shapes, their names, and the laundry list of skills they need in a matter of one hundred eighty days in a school year."

Parents, let that sink in for a moment. If your children can walk into a school knowing these foundational skills I just mentioned, you will set them up for success. Not to mention the assistance you will provide to the educators as they help you give your scholars a high-quality education. There are endless apps, videos, books, songs, etc. that can facilitate the learning of these foundational skills. Once you do your part, you'll be in a better position as the head of the home to hold school policymakers and administrators accountable for ensuring equitable education for your children, as they transition back and forth between your home and to the schoolhouse.

## CHAPTER TAKEAWAYS

In order for accountability to thrive, it needs to be nurtured with healthy attitudes, boundaries, and relationships.

- Maximize the teachable moments in your daily routines with your children because they will become the soundtracks, legacy clips, and heritage they pass down to the next generation.
- If you don't set boundaries for your kids in the virtual world, you will lose them in real life.
- Children will have more respect for you when you model the integrity and characteristics you want to pass down to them.

## PROBE AND TRANSFORM

What is stopping you from establishing a consistent daily routine at home for your children that includes designated study time, homework completion, and review sessions?

- Initiate conversations with your child about their school day, asking specific questions about what they learned, any challenges they faced, and their goals.
- How can you demonstrate a lifelong love for learning and personal growth by engaging in your own educational pursuits?
- How do you set clear expectations at home and school with your children? How are they monitored? Are there rewards and consequences for meeting or not meeting expectations?

# POLICYMAKERS

With each stroke of their pen, policymakers hold the potential to uplift or stifle, to empower or hinder.

# Bridge The Gaps

Let us dismantle inequity walls, brick by brick,
Learn to build bridges where divisions stick,
Bridge the gaps, the disparities are wide,
Equitable resources, let them coincide.
In every corner, diversity thrives,
Textbooks whisper stories of lives,
Representation blooms in every page,
Empathy nurtured at an early stage.
Resources abound, regardless of a zip code,
For quality education, a right bestowed.
From urban streets to the plush rural plains,
Ensure every child's success, no matter the terrains.
Reduce the burdens, the tests that weigh,
Nurturing curiosity, let students have their say,
Assessments fair, reflective of growth,
A holistic view, allowing each child to boast.
Embrace the arts, let creativity thrive,
Nurturing the soul, where passions come alive,
For music, dance, and colors unfurled,
Inspire imagination in every boy and girl.
Address biases that linger, firm and strong,
So everyone feels they truly belong
Parents, communities, stakeholders in one voice,
Creating a synergy where dreams rejoice.

# 4 | SETTING THE BAR

## *Respect* + Accountability = **Growth**

With each stroke of their pen, policymakers hold the potential to uplift or stifle, to empower or hinder. Your impact on education is significant, casting permanent skid marks that linger long after the ink has dried. It's no secret that diversity, equity, and inclusion were not included when education was created in America during the colonial period. Here we are, centuries later, still functioning on a biased infrastructure. Programs and policies have come and gone, revised and remixed only to maintain the same sound. There hasn't been a collective effort of manpower to uproot the system and replant it on fertile grounds to make it more fruitful. Until that happens, I dare to challenge you as a policymaker to call out the elephant in the room, have uncomfortable conversations, and dismantle every problematic issue piece by piece.

It is widely acknowledged that effective educational policies and laws are essential for creating a robust and equitable education system. However, the United States has faced numerous challenges in this regard. The first roadblock I'd like to address is inequitable funding. One of the most significant challenges in the American education system is the inequitable distribution of funding among schools. According to a report by the US Department of Education, high-poverty districts receive significantly less funding per student compared to low-poverty districts. This disparity hinders the ability of schools in disadvantaged areas to provide quality education. I've worked at many schools that experienced this injustice. It was sickening, sitting in professional development district trainings with colleagues who worked at schools in nearby cities where students sat in the lap of luxuries while the students I served were using very minimal resources.

To address the issue of inequitable funding, policymakers should prioritize a fair funding formula that accounts for the varying needs of different district schools. This can be achieved by allocating additional resources to economically disadvantaged areas, ensuring that all students have access to quality educational opportunities. Evidence from states like New Jersey, which implemented a progressive-funding model, shows that equitable funding can improve student achievement and narrow achievement gaps.

Another critical issue is the overemphasis on standardized testing, which has led to a narrowing of the curriculum and reduced focus on critical thinking and creativity. The No Child Left Behind Act, introduced in 2001, exacerbated this problem by mandating annual testing in core subjects. This has resulted in a teach-to-the-test culture, stifling students' holistic development and limiting teachers' autonomy. To alleviate the overemphasis on standardized testing, a shift towards a balanced assessment system is necessary. This system should incorporate a range of assessment methods, including performance-based assessments, portfolios, and teacher evaluations. By measuring students' holistic growth and capturing their diverse skills and talents, educators can foster a well-rounded education. States like New Hampshire have implemented competency-based assessments, allowing students to demonstrate proficiency in various areas beyond traditional tests. Better yet, allocate the testing funds to opportunities for experiential learning so students can gain the hands-on experiences and life skills they desperately need.

As a result of educators being battered and feeling disempowered for so long, they've been leaving the profession at an alarming rate.

Educational policies often fail to provide adequate support and professional development opportunities for teachers. Many educators feel overwhelmed by standardized testing, administrative burdens, lack of resources, and limited opportunities for growth. The brain drain is causing classrooms to be filled with college-educated adults who are not trained in pedagogy and child development, which creates additional problems. Schools and corporations are feeling the wrath of educational injustices. To improve the quality of education, policymakers should prioritize comprehensive teacher support and professional development. This includes reducing administrative burdens, increasing access to resources, and providing ongoing training opportunities. Evidence suggests that investing in high-quality professional development programs improves teaching practices and positively impacts student outcomes. Connecticut has implemented a comprehensive support system, including mentoring programs and targeted professional development, resulting in increased teacher satisfaction and retention.

Lastly, educators should be respected and valued, especially when it comes to compensation. Education is the only profession that shapes and molds every professional in the world. No other profession in the world comes close to this noble and necessary task. As a result, it's disheartening that educators are not compensated for the hard and essential work they do. Instead of being one of, if not, the highest paid professionals, most teachers are left to additional part-time jobs to make ends meet, thus lowering their effectiveness in the classroom. It is crucial to prioritize evidence-based solutions and engage in ongoing dialogue to ensure that educational policies align with the needs of students, teachers, and society as a whole.

Public education in America, like any institution, is not immune to biases. Several biases and inequities exist within the education system, affecting students from different backgrounds. Racial and ethnic biases persist in various aspects of education, including discipline practices, access to advanced courses, and resource allocation. Studies have shown that students of color, particularly black and Hispanic students, are disproportionately disciplined, suspended, or expelled compared to their white counterparts for similar infractions. Additionally, there is often a lack of representation and cultural responsiveness in curriculum and teaching materials, which can marginalize students from diverse backgrounds.

One effective strategy to mitigate this issue is by implementing curriculum and instructional practices that reflect and value students' diverse cultures and backgrounds. This should include accurate literature, historical narratives, and scientific discoveries from different cultures. All educators should undergo cultural diversity training in order to raise awareness of biases, challenge stereotypes, and develop culturally sensitive teaching strategies. More importantly, all educators should be well-versed on how to create environments that respect diverse perspectives and properly educate on equity, diversity, and inclusion.

Socioeconomic bias is another cancerous practice that needs to be uprooted, because the disparities contribute to educational biases. Students from low-income families often face challenges related to inadequate resources, limited access to extracurricular activities, and lower-quality schools. These issues can perpetuate the achievement gap, as students from economically disadvantaged backgrounds may not receive the same educational opportunities as their wealthier peers. Combatting socioeconomic bias in public school is a long-term and comprehensive commitment. As mentioned before, adequate funding is necessary to support services that help mitigate the needs. This can include hiring qualified staff, providing targeted interventions, offering mental and health-care services, and improving infrastructure and facilities. In essence, it has to be a wraparound approach if we really want to address the academic and non-academic barriers to learning.

Later in the book, we'll take a deeper dive into some of the other areas like family and community engagement, accountability, collaborative partnerships, and curriculum approaches.

Students with disabilities often face biases and inequities within the education system. There have been instances of overrepresentation or underrepresentation of certain groups within special-education programs, indicating potential biases in identifying and assessing students' needs.

Additionally, inadequate resources and support for students with disabilities can hinder their educational progress. This issue is bigger than creating equitable policies and ensuring strict enforcement. It's about being intentional when allocating funding to train educators on how to implement differentiated practices and behavior management methods.

In addition, school staff should have access to assistive technologies as essential accommodations to meet the unique needs of students with disabilities. In the same vein, there has to be a more effective system that addresses the travesty of disproportionate identification of students, especially as it pertains to certain racial and ethnic backgrounds.

I can attest that this is a serious concern for the community I was raised in. Growing up in Haiti, there was no special education system. When Haitian parents with limited ability to speak English sit in placement meetings for their children, more often than not they sign papers and agree to terms they know nothing about. Over my two decades of experience in education, I've been fortunate to have been a translator for some parents during these meetings and was able to help mitigate a world of misunderstandings. I can assure you there are thousands who have had the misfortune of navigating that dark space all alone. I'm not sure what type of monitoring and evaluation systems are currently in place, but I guarantee they are not as effective as they need to be. Our students are struggling, and the quality of services is not up to par.

As a former English language learner (ELL) who migrated to the United States at the age of ten, I faced a number of challenges that included, but were not limited to, language barriers and cultural differences. The concerns and solutions are very similar to those of special education, which were mentioned in the previous paragraph. An additional layer of support should be the provision of adequate resources and support for language acquisition and proficiency development. This ranges from qualified teachers and support staff to effective cultural competency programs.

There is a dire need to establish mechanisms for monitoring and holding schools accountable for addressing ELL bias. This can include regular data collection, analysis of ELL student outcomes, and implementing measures to address disparities or inequities in access to quality education. A big part of the solution is to fund anti-bias training for school staff to raise awareness of unconscious biases and stereotypes that may impact ELL students. A number of ELL students are neglected in classrooms, because untrained teachers either give them some sort of technology software to babysit their so-called learning or ignore them altogether. This type of educational injustice is not acceptable. There has to be greater accountability. Funding and mandating strategic training and strategies will help create a more inclusive and equitable learning environment.

Policymakers play a critical role in addressing reforms and biases in schools. It's crucial to enforce diverse representation in teaching staff, leadership positions, and curriculum materials to provide role models and perspectives that reflect the student population. Lastly, policymakers should promote and incentivize inclusive practices that support the education of scholars with accommodations. This should include the use of a universal design for learning and mandating collaboration between general and special education educators in order to provide proper support. Since learning is a lifelong journey, education should reflect a continual evolution driven by societal needs, breakthroughs, advancements, and necessary reforms. As policymakers, you play a pivotal role in this ongoing process. I implore you to dig deeper into collaborating with educators and communities to strive to create an equitable and effective education system for all students and families.

## CHAPTER TAKEAWAYS

With each stroke of their pen, policymakers hold the potential to uplift or stifle, to empower or hinder.

- Allocate additional resources to economically disadvantaged areas, ensuring ALL students have access to quality educational opportunities.
- Implement curriculum and instructional practices that reflect and value students' diverse cultures and backgrounds.
- Dig deeper into collaborating with educators and communities to strive to create an equitable and effective education system for all students and families.

## PROBE AND TRANSFORM

What strategies can policymakers implement to attract and retain highly qualified and motivated teachers in public schools?

- What steps should policymakers take to promote critical thinking, problem-solving, and creativity in the curriculum, moving away from rote memorization and standardized testing?
- How should policymakers allocate resources to ensure adequate funding for public education, including infrastructure improvements, instructional materials, technology, digital resources, and student support services?
- What policies should be implemented to address the achievement gap between different student populations, such as racial and ethnic minorities, English language learners, and students with disabilities?

# PRINCIPALS

**Schools fail or flourish at the feet and leadership of administration.**

# Caring Administrator

Parents plant, principals help water the seeds
From homes to schools, young minds bloom
Germinating knowledge as each child succeeds
Absorbing as much skill as they can consume.
School is a garden where minds grow
The soil is saturated with care
The administrator is gardener who must sow
Seeds of knowledge, equity, and a passion to share.
With a steady hand, the principal must lead
Inspire teachers to reach new heights
Listen and partner with the community, and take heed
Of the students' needs and brighten their lights.
A great leader is more than a boss
They are a mentor, coach, and a friend
Who will love, encourage, and never cause
Fear or doubt in the hearts that they tend.

# 5 | FAIL OR FLOURISH

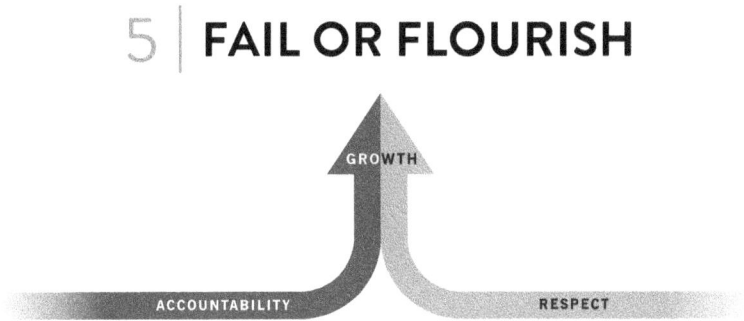

## *Respect* + Accountability = **Growth**

S chools fail or flourish at the feet and leadership of administration. One of the things I've witnessed is that schools consistently follow the energy of their leaders. Just as parents lead their homes to prepare children for learning, administrators are responsible for leading the charge of preparing a team of adults to impact scholars and families. It is not an easy task! As a former reading coach and assistant principal, I had the privilege of sitting in meetings with courageous visionaries and was fortunate to have seen their perspectives on the educational landscape. It is a fact that being a principal is a demanding role that comes with numerous challenges and complexities. They encounter an immense amount of stress due to the huge responsibilities they bear. They're challenged with balancing expectations from state legislators, district administrators, parents, teachers, and others. Not to mention balancing budgets, resolving conflicts, implementing policies, disciplining staff members, and addressing sensitive issues. This is in addition to whatever may be going in their personal lives.

Administrators, I definitely understand your struggles. These mountainous hurdles can lead to feelings of isolation, emotional exhaustion, and burnout. Principals who place importance on self-care demonstrate higher levels of emotional resilience and a greater ability to manage the challenges inherent in their roles. Self-care practices, such as regular exercise, seeking social support, and engaging in hobbies, have been associated with decreased stress levels and increased job satisfaction among principals (Grayson and Alvarez 2008). By practicing self-care, principals can enhance their own well-being, reduce burnout, and ultimately lead schools more effectively, creating a positive impact on the entire school community. Courageous leaders, I'd like to encourage you to seek that healthy balance you desperately deserve.

I believe there are three common traits among successful administrators that need to be implemented in order to lead a thriving school: the ability to create culture, build relationships, and prepare leaders. Before principals are hired to lead schools, they must know the type of culture they want to create. Before you can build relationships, you must establish your educational philosophy, vision, and mission. In doing so, the goals and decisions you make will reinforce where you plan on taking the school as an equitable leader who seeks to create thriving learning environments. Once you've solidified the latter, be prepared to clearly articulate it to your staff. Word of advice, it behooves you to be approachable, firm, and fair. I totally understand that principals have different entry points and challenges when they start their administrative assignments, but be mindful of how you address your staff. After all, they're going to be your front-line soldiers once the bell rings on the first day of school, so be kind. I've been under the leadership of a principal who felt the need to let us know that she was the one in charge. I don't know if it was the Napoleon complex because she was vertically challenged, but she rubbed the entire staff the wrong way. She fought an unnecessary uphill battle her first year at the school because of the ineffective way she initially approached her staff. Great leaders don't get married to titles, because they are wise enough to understand that it's the people on their team who really matter.

## Creating Culture

Research suggests that creating a positive school culture is essential for principals, as it can have a significant impact on student achievement, teacher retention, and school safety. Those are arguably the top three components of any school. Culture has to be inclusive with a clear message that all hands need to be on deck. As the top leader in the school, your job is to build the capacity of everyone working under you. They all should see and experience growth at the end of the school year. Each team member needs to feel a sense of belonging and ownership in their respective roles. At the end of the day, whatever they're responsible for matters! In order for the school as a whole to be effective, each person needs to do their job and stay in their lanes at all times. Ultimately, quality education does more than provide students access to become successful; it also transforms society as a whole. What better way to impact the world than to start with revolutionizing your school as your mini-society.

Every department needs to be engaged, from administrative assistants to janitorial workers. One of the best ways to do so is to have an online tool like Google Forms for each department leader and its staff to provide feedback on what's working and what's not throughout the school year. An additional step could be to have them craft possible solutions to the issues they notice. Either the principal or assistant principal need to meet with the department heads on a regular basis to review the "glows" and "grows." It's crucial to be clear to every employee that every idea won't come to fruition, but they will be discussed and considered. This is important so no one gets offended if their suggestions don't become a reality. At the end of the day, decisions will be based on what's best for children and aligned with the culture the principal is establishing. Notice I say *establishing* because fluidity is important in a school setting with so many moving pieces. Having the wisdom and flexibility to pivot is paramount.

Every department needs to own the fact that they are all educators. For instance, the janitorial staff is vital to the school's landscape and cleanliness. It gives first impressions about the school before a visitor engages in a conversation with a staff member. It can determine whether or not parents allow their babies to spend seven to eight hours on a particular campus. The fact that schools are one of the germiest places to work, a clean environment protects the health of everyone in the building. This will help prevent the spread of infectious diseases, which in turn reduces absenteeism. Studies have confirmed that students perform better in tidy schools. Imagine having the janitorial staff provide biweekly or monthly tips to the school body on how to better maintain a clean school? A report by the *American School & University* magazine notes that janitors also play an important role in promoting positive school culture. The report highlights how janitors who build positive relationships with students and staff can contribute to a more positive school climate and help reduce disciplinary problems (*American School & University* 2019).

Additionally, the head of security or resource officer can also provide support and tips on a regular basis. These things can be done through newsletters, morning announcements, or classroom visits. They can serve as guest speakers or do Read Alouds for students. These in-house adults are prime check-in mentors to scholars because they have access to them daily. This is also possible with secretaries, counselors, paraprofessionals, and any adult working in your professional setting.

Looking back at my career, I realized that I organically created good rapport with the janitorial staff, office staff, security guards, and other valuable individuals who are typically overlooked when it comes to educating our students. I've learned so much about their stories and the vast amount of value they possess. Their wisdom made me a better educator. After all, every worker in the school sat in a classroom at some point in their lifetime.

Similarly, there are children in your building who are wired to excel in the various positions on your campus. I believe every school, from primary to secondary, should have Career Day at least three times a year. The first one should only include professionals who are in-house because they represent such diversity. The event will not only guarantee positive school culture, but it will also create a sense of belonging and engagement school wide. Empowering students with the mindset that they can start out as a janitor and work towards owning a company that provides well-trained janitors to multiple schools is a motivational hack that will impact their work ethic in the classroom. It's no secret that every scholar at your school will not go to college, so why not engage and expose them to various options early and often. At the end of the day, your job as a principal is to create a culture that uplifts and empowers every living soul who will spend ten months of the year under your supervision.

## Building Relationships

Once the vision for school culture is clear, it is vital for principals to hire the right people and understand how to maximize the potential of all staff members. A good starting point is to seek qualified individuals who are already doing what your vision entails. I've had the privilege of sitting in on a number of interviews with teacher candidates. I must say, people will tell exactly who they are as long as you ask the right questions. Some interviews lasted fifteen minutes while others ran well over an hour. We made some good choices, but unfortunately, we also picked some bad apples. Looking back, I believe that our faux pas had everything to do with not sticking to the culture we wanted to create.

I understand that education is in a state of crisis in terms of being understaffed. The brain drain in the profession is disheartening. I would encourage you, as the top leader, to choose quality over quantity. As long as you create an effective game plan with your leadership team and staff that will help you maintain until you get the right people in the right places, you will make it. Until then, do your best not to compromise the standard you set for the individuals who will be responsible for shaping and molding the vulnerable young people at your school. I understand that you may inherit some bad apples when you accept your principal position. I implore you to clearly lay out your vision, get to know their strengths, weaknesses, and give them some time to adjust and adapt. If they're not a good match, be honest with them. Give them some options and be honest with yourself in determining whether or not they're a good fit. They may be the right person in the wrong position or at the wrong school.

At my first full-time job as an educator, I worked at an elementary school under a phenomenal principal. That man had his finger on the pulse of everyone and everything at the school. He had his vision, he understood data, and he maximized the skills of the entire staff. It was clear that no one should get comfortable in their positions, which is pretty common at the elementary level. Of course, there were those who didn't like him because he was upfront and decisive. At the same time, every move he made was about enhancing the educational experience of every student in the building. He was a champion for collaboration, building staff capacity, and maximizing abilities. One year, I went from teaching reading comprehension skills in Haitian-Creole in small groups, to moving from class to class with Haitian students who were new to the country, to assisting with state-standardized writing clinics, to co-teaching a reading class. All of this was possible because he got to know me during the interview process and utilized my strengths to help him move the needle towards fulfilling the vision he had for the school. During his tenure, the school went from a failing school to an A, double-A, and triple-A school. I'm not a big fan of standardized testing and school grades; I only used that example because those results were indicative of the transformation and growth that happened on every level.

Relationships are the heartbeat of human beings. We have been wired to live and thrive in community. As a matter of fact, relationships are linked to a wide range of positive outcomes, including better mental and physical health, increased happiness and well-being, and improved academic and behavioral outcomes in children. Not prioritizing this innate need that is embedded in every living soul is counterproductive for a leader. As a principal, on a scale of one to ten, how would you rate your ability to foster healthy relationships among all staff at your school? I'm not talking about the shallow ideology of hoping it happens. I'm referring to the intentionality of making sure staff members connect and collaborate in meaningful ways that will transfer into a rich learning environment for the young minds at your school. Additionally, the morale and creativity will mesh and explode into eclectic results. This will automatically boost productivity among students and staff members, which translates to what has become the lifeline of the profession, obtaining successful data. Building strong relationships is at the root of these landmarks. Adults are just like the students, if they don't like you or believe you care, they won't work for you.

Before I became a teacher, I was blessed to experience the power of building strong relationships on a team. I was a student athlete from high school to college. Thankfully, I had a chance to be part of winning teams at a high level. There were some common practices from the variety of coaches I had: we failed and succeeded as one, we spent time together outside of sports, we were accountable for one another, and we pushed each other to be better every day. As a result, I was part of undefeated teams, conference-winning champions, and nationally ranked programs. Most importantly, we won both on and off the field, because the discipline of cultivating relationships is a skill that we acquired for life.

When I became a teacher, it was natural for me to seek a mentor, because I wanted to be better. This is well before I learned about how mentoring programs help reduce teacher turnover and improve student learning outcomes. I had principals who were strategic about placing me under the leadership of experienced educators, so they could teach me the ropes. I became a sponge in those situations. A study published in the *Journal of Teacher Education* found that mentorship programs can help to increase the professional development and job satisfaction of both beginning and experienced teachers (Darling-Hammond et al. 2009).

First and foremost, as the principal, you have to create a good plan with realistic expectations. Before you can adhere to lofty district goals and state scores, you'll have to focus on how you are going to train your inexperienced and uncertified teachers. According to The American Association of Colleges for Teacher Education, the number of people completing a teacher education program has been declining dramatically in the past decade. Not to mention that recent surveys have shown that over 50 percent of teachers are thinking about leaving the field. Having said that, I believe your battlefield is to leverage the rock-star educators in your building who are committed to the work, approach them about being mentors, and be strategic about professional development to build their capacity and those of the newbies. If your teacher data doesn't move, it's highly unlikely for your school data to improve. Moreover, be sure to add a solid layer of Positive Behavioral Interventions and Supports (PBIS), because classroom management has to be solidified in order for effective learning to take place. Similar to culture, it has to be implemented with fidelity. Without consistency, teaching and learning will be a calamity.

Building a solid rapport with your educators is the most pivotal relationship you need to nourish in your school. They should be an extension of you, because they have the most contact hours with the students. No one on campus can roll out your vision and philosophy better than the educators. They are your franchise players. There is no school without teachers. Like the students, there need to be incentives in place for them as well. During my second year as an assistant principal, our administration team decided to gift all teachers with in-house planning day every quarter to help them catch up and collaborate. We had them sign up for different days, hired substitutes, and gave them a space to work. They utilized the time to grade papers, plan ahead, observe their colleagues teach, and meet with content coaches. They were so appreciative and felt encouraged because it helped them plan, grow, and collaborate. My principal and I taught at the same school for a few years and would frequently converse about a few things that our bosses could do differently. Less than five years later, we teamed up as administrators and began to implement some of the things we wished we had when we were in the classroom. As I mentioned before, it's an effective practice to get input from your staff. They have ideas that can make your job easier and help you grow as an effective leader. After all, if you're going to spend time and money to hire smart people on your team, you have to let them utilize their intelligence.

Backwards planning is a concept that can be used to motivate your teachers. It'll be wise to make it a practical concept during the school year for their lesson planning.

Here's a tangible example. A friend of mine works for a private firm that gives their employees fake money for reaching milestones and working in excellence. At the end of the year, they host an auction where everyone is able to bid on various items. The prizes ranged from paid time off to $1000 vacation vouchers. Of course, the people who earned the most funds during the course of the year were able to bid on and win the more luxurious prizes. I wish I knew about this when I was an administrator. This is something that can be customized to your liking. Essentially, it's giving your staff an incentive to look forward to. Because our beloved educators are severely underpaid, anytime we can add value to the workday is a huge win.

Celebrations and meals are great ways to ensure culture and relationship building remain consistent. During the course of the year, there are a great deal of cultural celebrations that need to be acknowledged with mini-celebrations and food. You know people love free food! I'm sure most of your staff consist of people from various parts of the world who are dying to share their heritage. It will create a sense of belonging and intimacy with the diverse population of children and families in your building. I've hosted and helped produce a ton of Haitian Flag Day celebrations at every school I worked at. As a matter of fact, those celebrations inspired me to author a bilingual children's book series about Haitian history.

Celebrating children's success in the classroom at the end of an assignment or project is another powerful way of bringing people together. For example, you can support an educator who decides to turn the classroom into an art gallery with students' finished work. Light snacks for school staff and guardians can be ordered for the community as they indulge and peruse the scholars' artwork. These types of experiences are significant.

I'll leave you with one more example of a project one of my principals cosigned on that made a huge impact on students and their families. I was working on a unit with my students on the Harlem Renaissance. The scholars wrote poems, songs, created artwork and dances, as they responded to the monumental era in African American history. They worked hard and were eager to share their original works with the community. I went a step above by proposing to my principal that she rent a local venue to host the event. She agreed! Parents and the school community came out for an evening of inspiring artistic expression and good food! Years later, some of my former students were still reminiscing about that experience.

As a teacher, I didn't look forward to faculty meetings. After a long day of working with children, I don't know too many educators who salivate over that hour. However, I've seen food and music incorporated into those meetings to make them more pleasurable. I'm talking about simple snacks and festive tunes before jumping into data talks. If you have the budget for it, go ahead and do it big! After a long day of teaching, those little things make a huge difference. I confess, that was one of my weaknesses when I became an administrator. I was not into those little details. Thank God for people around me who were, because they would constantly remind me about it.

If you're like me, I would suggest delegating that leadership task to a staff member who enjoys hospitality. Trust me, there's always one on every team. Some schools have sunshine committees that handle these types of events. Ultimately, the goal is to look at the systems that are already in place at your school and maximize them by finding ways to create better relationships and culture for the people you are leading.

## Building Leaders

An educator who had been in the classroom for over fifteen years was astonished when I uttered these words to her: "My job is to prepare you to replace me." As a veteran teacher for well over a decade, she exclaimed she had never heard someone in leadership approach an educator that way.

To be honest, I was a bit alarmed as well, because I didn't realize such a practice was rare. The more teachers I spoke to, the more their stories aligned with their lack of leaders who were intentionally looking to work themselves out of a position. I was blessed to have had the privilege to be under the leadership of one of my principals who wanted to build me up to levels that were beyond my aspirations. I wholeheartedly believe that there are a massive number of leaders like yourself who want to do the same thing for your staff. The problem may be that your message may not be as intentional and clear. As the head of school, it's paramount that you are strategic and vocal about building leadership skills in both your staff and students. By doing so, you will remove unnecessary barriers and build trust with your community that you are invested in their growth personally and professionally.

If that is not your intention as an administrator, it would be wise for you to do a heart and bias check. I would go as far as saying you may consider another profession. This line of work has everything to do with uplifting people. If that doesn't run through your veins, you will not be as successful as you need to be as a leader. Consequently, a school without strong adult leaders who are committed to creating a culture that is conducive to high achievement will not achieve academic success.

Do you know your staff's aspirations? Have you ever taken that kind of inventory? It's a data point that can be extremely helpful in shaping leaders at your school. A simple Google Forms survey is all you need. Once I transitioned into a leadership role, I asked every single person I worked with to let me know what their ultimate career goals were. That was important for me to know, because I communicated to them that I wanted to do everything I could to help them reach their targets. I also used that information to drive lesson plan conversations and class projects. When people are functioning in their sweet spots by doing something they enjoy, the work is gratifying. It's also effective to be aware of their ambitions because it will help with professional development and partnerships that will be beneficial to the school body.

Seeing the gifts and potential in each person is powerful. Knowing your teachers' strengths and objectives will enable you to create professional leaders and learners. Earlier I mentioned how I was part of an administrative team that gifted teachers the opportunity to do informal peer observations. Such a structure lent itself to spotlighting evidence-based practices among the staff. One year, we had one of our science teachers lead a professional development session on systems and routines she used effectively. This is a great way to develop leadership skills. Not to mention that teachers spend more time with each other and tend to trust one another more than they trust their administrators. So it would be wise for you to leverage those bonds to maximize your school's growth as you strive to build deeper relationships yourself with your colleagues.

Mentorship is an evidence-based practice that can shift the culture of your school, nurture social emotional and academic learning, and breed healthy leaders. Most importantly, if this is done correctly, it will improve student achievement. Fortunately, brain research has confirmed that social, emotional, and academic learning are interconnected. In many ways, organic mentorship may be taking place at your school. That's great. I want to encourage you to make it schoolwide. As a principal, you should naturally pour into the lives of your assistant principals to be able to be better than you when they reach your position. In turn, they should be doing the same with the coaches. As a leadership unit, you should make room to create opportunities for teachers who aspire to be school leaders. That's a formula that will guarantee success and sustainability long after you step down from your position.

As adults are supporting each other, every single staff member should be engaged in mentoring students. I get it. You may have people on your campus who make you cringe and hesitate to pair with one of your precious scholars. Before you go off on a tangent and start thinking about how counterproductive it'll be to have those individuals pour into the lives of young people, I want you to consider how the process may be transformational.

The power of accountability has a way to convict the heart, fix crooked steps, and lead individuals down a straight path. When people are placed in a position to consistently encourage others and give good advice, it will make them reflect on their personal lives. Give everyone on your staff a chance, and let them determine whether or not they are responsible enough to be trusted. There are amazing stories and nuggets of wisdom in the minds and hearts of your school community leaders that are dormant and not being maximized. I would go as far as saying, some of the withheld information can be a matter of life and death. Let your staff pour life into one another. Don't get me wrong, if it's clear that a particular adult is too toxic to help lead a few minors, he or she doesn't need to be part of your team. It sounds harsh, but it has to be that way in order to build a healthy environment.

I know you may be wondering: with everything you're responsible for as a principal, when will you have time to oversee a mentorship program? Better yet, how high will it rank on your infinite to-do list? I'm glad you asked, because it's a task that can be delegated to a responsible individual on your campus who's willing and looking to build leadership capacity. All you do is ask and have him or her report to you biweekly or monthly. Once there is a point person or two to facilitate the process, getting started becomes easier. Every school is different, every environment is unique, so tailor your program accordingly. You may have staff members who are already doing the work and simply need to merge it with your framework, while others may need more assistance. It can be structured simply by creating a spreadsheet with all the students' names, sending an email link to every adult, and having them select the prescribed number of scholars.

I remember spearheading something similar at a school I worked at. The adults and their mentees had weekly check-ins, which included talks about goal settings, academic progress, challenges, and successes. Once a month, pizza was provided for the mentors to break bread with the students. This process was implemented for half of the school year and repeated for the second half with the adults choosing a different set of children.

As a side note, please connect with your counselors and mental health professionals on campus to create clear expectations and boundaries in order to protect everyone involved. Unfortunately, we have to acknowledge the fact that some students and teachers have crossed boundary lines and wrecked many lives. Lastly, I'm fully aware that there are some established district and nationwide mentorship programs that are supporting schools. While they're effective in their own rights, I still believe in-house mentorship is more powerful because the day-to-day interaction with students will have a greater impact in the long run.

Another mentorship tactic that is efficient in fostering deep relationships and leadership skills between adults and students is advisory. An advisory is an inclusive and equitable learning community that consists of an adult and a small group of students, preferably no more than ten. It's designed to build a student's sense of voice, safety, and ability to take ownership of their learning and shape their school experience. Again, this can be done on a whole school approach or student and teacher approach. The idea is to carve ten to fifteen minutes, preferably at the beginning of the school day, where the grade-level groups meet frequently with one adult advisor. There, they'll create a mini-village that provides accountability.

A well-facilitated advisory has endless benefits. Pre-teach, pre-teach, and pre-teach before you roll out this process. Show videos to students and staff so they can see what it looks like, sounds like, and feels like. Then, facilitate conversation to make sure everyone understands their roles and the value they will add to the process. Once training and support are provided, the adults can hone their leadership skills by implementing an established advisory curriculum. Yes, curriculums already exist for this kind of work, so you do not need to reinvent the wheel. Of course, some aspects can be tailored to your school, but no need to put extra work on your staff. A good curriculum targets social, emotional, and academic growth. Another benefit of advisory is it creates a sense of family within each group that enables them to have a greater sense of belonging and support as they track their progress along the way. This safe space can also be a medium that helps young people resolve conflicts in a healthier manner and learn how to make better decisions. Advisory is a win-win concept as it develops leadership skills in both staff and scholars.

You are the principal. You have the noble task of spearheading transformation for generations to come. It is a hefty but fulfilling charge.

Your oversight of school operations directly impacts the optimization of successful communities. You were built for this type of work. You have to build it on a solid foundation for it to work effectively. Before you herald your master plan to the neighborhood, you must have a treatment for your curriculum and how it is going to cure the ills of a fractured educational society.

## CHAPTER TAKEAWAYS

Principals who place importance on self-care demonstrate higher levels of emotional resilience and a greater ability to manage the challenges inherent in their roles.

- Schools fail or flourish at the feet and leadership of administration.
- Creating a positive school culture is essential for principals, as it can have a significant impact on student achievement, teacher retention, and school safety.
- Healthy relationships help people connect and collaborate in meaningful ways.
- Without consistency, teaching and learning will be a calamity.

## PROBE AND TRANSFORM

How can principals foster a positive and inclusive school culture that values diversity, respect, and collaboration among students, staff, and parents?

- What strategies can principals employ to provide ongoing mentorship and coaching opportunities for emerging staff leaders to nurture a culture of leadership development?
- What measures can principals implement to address conflicts or challenges within the school community?
- How can principals initiate regular and meaningful communication channels with students, staff, and parents to foster open and trusting relationships?

# Collaborative Leader

Principals possess the power to push

For school progress by leveraging families,

Curriculum, and community to craft a culture

That nurtures growth, grit, and ingenuity.

With passion and purpose, they promote

Robust and remote systems to reach students

With a riveting roar to enrich minds down to the core.

Families are the foundation that stand firm.

They are the roots that run deep.

They are the connections between campus
and community

That foster partnerships to take people to
thriving places.

Collaboration makes learning come alive with love and
lasting legacy.

When principals create curriculum with families
and community

Students flourish, teachers become first-class educators.

Parents will see schools as a second home, a harmonious safe haven

With vigorous core values they envisioned for
their families.

# 6 | FLUID AND INCLUSIVE SCHOOL

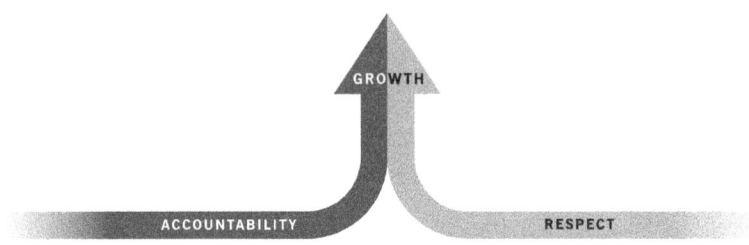

## *Respect* **+** Accountability **= Growth**

I t's no secret that the educational system in America is functioning on a biased infrastructure. The foundation was laid with a structure that prohibited black children from receiving an education. It graduated to biased integration that was grounded in an avalanche of disparities towards minorities. The COVID-19 pandemic exacerbated the racial imbalances that exist in schools. Student opportunities and access to a robust education are based on income, race, and ethnicity among other things. Although schools in high-poverty areas that disproportionately educate children of color have the highest need, they somehow receive the least funding. Take a minute to digest that logic. The latter normally results in inadequate resources, facilities, and personnel.

For instance, according to the Centers for Disease Control and Prevention, elevated blood lead levels, which is caused by lead in drinking water, have been linked to hearing and speech problems, brain and nervous system damage, learning disabilities, and decreased growth. This is an issue that has been found exclusively in low-income communities. It's safe to say that those black and brown children are living compromised lives, in every aspect of the word. A significant number of schools in marginalized areas are faced with buildings in dire need of repair, underserved children, and historically biased information in classroom books. As a principal, this is the predicament you're inheriting. Until the powers that be decide to blow up the educational framework and rebuild it with an equitable foundation, it is unrealistic for anyone to expect you to remedy all of these issues at once. However, you are in a position to impact some changes in your curriculum, family engagement, and community involvement.

## Robust Curriculum

Curriculum implementation is one of the most important components you inherit as a principal. Parents send their babies to your building to receive skills and content that will help them become future change agents. In order to meet those needs, it's vital for you to know the community you're serving, and to prioritize their needs with the products and processes you expose them to. The vetted textbooks that are typically approved in schools are not enough.

I'm a product of Miami-Dade Public Schools District, a former classroom teacher, reading coach, and administrator for over twenty years. I can assure you that a vast majority of the cultural content I've acquired was learned on my own. Growing up in Little Haiti, a predominantly Haitian-populated community in Miami, no one taught me about the monumental impact my heritage had on America and across the world. No one taught me that what we now know as the city of Chicago was founded by Haitian businessman, Jean-Baptiste Point Du Sable. History books glossed over the Louisiana Purchase and did not include that it was possible, as a result of the only successful slave revolt in history when Haiti defeated France in 1803, to become the first free black republic in the world. We were exposed to Paul Revere's Midnight Ride but weren't told of Wentworth Cheswell, a black man who rode with Revere.

Every child deserves to know the truth about history and every topic they learn in school. More importantly, they need to see themselves in the educational journey. Curriculum is not a final product. It's a fluid, ongoing process. Children need to know that current events are connected to situations and decisions from centuries ago. Education needs to create the bridge that allows minds to travel back and forth to different eras to connect the dots. Every student, regardless of ethnic background, needs exposure to multicultural and social justice education. They need to know the true beliefs, perspectives, and values of people from various backgrounds. That is the only way they'll be equipped to uproot the detrimental practices their predecessors couldn't eradicate.

Once the vision for a school is established, curriculum design should be drafted by key leaders. This includes, but is not limited to, the assistant principal, department heads, and content coaches. Their input will ensure that alignment is maximized vertically and horizontally. Again, I want to reiterate that curriculum development is not static. It is a fluid and living process that evolves with time. Solidifying the framework is vital, but it should remain in a continuous state of refinement. As the leader, once you understand the community you're serving, marry it with your vision and mission for your school. You should put on your equity lens to create a curriculum that focuses on content that ignites deeper academic, social, and emotional learning. In doing so, scholars will be equipped with a good mix of culture, race, power, and life skills.

Chances are, you're probably not going to find all of those elements in one vendor or textbook, so you'll have to supplement with additional resources that are sound. Some of the said supplements may not cost you a dime. We'll explore those a little bit later in the book. The goal is to create systems and practices that will be implemented and measured to achieve high outcomes for all students, which should be designed to shape their lives beyond the four walls of your campus.

Curriculum gaps are like lizards: they live everywhere. They're in every state, district, and school. Your job is to do a gap analysis with your team to determine which one you want to prioritize. The issue lies between where you are and where you want to be. The hole can exist in school culture, student engagement, lesson preparation, lesson design, or lesson delivery just to name a few. The more courageous conversations your team engages in, the better prepared you'll be. As you're sitting in your war room, look around. If the curriculum development leaders who are sitting at your decision table do not match the representation of your student population, you have a personnel gap that needs to be addressed before you dive into the work. Diverse perspectives are absolutely essential for an effective curriculum.

In the latter part of my teaching career, I accepted a job at a startup school. I remember how excited I was when I was afforded the opportunity to write my own curriculum map. Prior to that, I worked at a traditional district school that was very structured. Although some of my previous administrators were flexible enough to allow me to be creative, I still felt stifled. The opportunity to craft my school-year journey was a dream come true. Granted, I had no experience designing a curriculum, but I had many years dissecting and poking holes into the cookie-cutter pacing guides that were assigned to me annually.

Either way, the opportunity taught me a lot. I had some wins and losses, but I grew! Although the students in my class performed well every year, their performances in other content areas were inconsistent. Honestly, I believe they could have done a lot better in my course if I would've thoroughly designed the curriculum with all the content teachers. Yes, we were given the framework and encouraged to collaborate, but the effort could've been more intentional. We had some smart, caring, and hard-working educators who had good intentions, but we needed more than our ad hoc efforts to be able to maximize the desired outcomes.

At the end of the day, the purpose of a curriculum is to engage all staff in implementing the principal's vision with common language, tools, time, and the consistency to strive for academic excellence. One year, I worked under a leader who exemplified the latter. He created a stipend for designated school leaders to meet on Saturdays two months prior to the end of the school year to plan the curriculum for the following year. The time was focused, the work was phenomenal, and the results spoke for themselves. Despite being an underfunded school in a low-income neighborhood, the school consistently outperformed the majority of "high-performing" schools in Miami-Dade County during my former principal's tenure.

Curriculums are the bridges that connect where you are as a school to where you'd like to be. As leader of your school, if you want to afford your scholars the possibility of making it to the other side, you have to be strategic in taking the necessary steps to form an effective team that will help you design an equitable curriculum that is well aligned with your vision.

## Amplify Parents' Voices

If you are going to hold families accountable for their children's education, you have to intentionally involve them in the educational process. You can no longer have guardians listen to what you think is best for them—rather, give them a platform to share their stories and concerns. The only way to truly hear their voices is to allow them to speak and share their narratives. Neuroscience has proven that storytelling is one of the most powerful ways to engage human beings and pass on pertinent knowledge across cultures and generations. This confirms that it is vital for schools to engage parents by finding common ground, celebrating them, and leveraging their knowledge.

Parents' experiences and voices have to be amplified and implemented. This is more powerful than any set of ideologies, systems, or processes we can come up with. I spent my entire educational career working in schools in low-income communities. It has been a pleasure to give back to the community that helped shape and build me into who I am today. However, I was disheartened to hear colleagues adopt a negative perception that low-income families do not care about their children's education. Nothing can be further from the truth. As a matter of fact, I've never met parents who sent their children to school without the desire to see their young people succeed. Having said that, one of the things that can be done to debunk the latter is to have parents share their expectations, values, and visions with schools.

Although my Haitian parents weren't familiar with the American school system when I was growing up, the standard for excellent education was always high. They weren't afforded the opportunity to share their stories with the schools we attended, but they made sure they verbalized their goals to us on a regular basis. They reminded us that even though they didn't have the privilege of earning an education beyond the secondary level, their choices were living sacrifices for us to be in a position to live better lives. They took it a step further by randomly showing up to the school to check on us. Their presence spoke for itself. They didn't have the language, but their actions communicated their level of commitment and expectations.

Trust me, I'm fully aware that some students do not come from a two-parent stable home like I did, but I've also been a part of school communities that supported young people who were facing challenging situations. Although we didn't have much, the fact that we had two involved parents made us feel like unicorns in the hood. Most of our neighbors were single-parent families. As a high school student, I witnessed coaches and educators step up to fill colossal gaps in the lives of some of my classmates, which helped them rise above their circumstances.

As a teacher, I've been part of a school that was able to identify students in dire need, communicate with the guardians, and provide food and care packages on a regular basis that were donated by local organizations. I'm confident there are thousands of similar stories among educators across the country. The charge for you, as the leader of your school, is to normalize that process.

Let's be clear, absent parents exist in both low-income and affluent communities. While the upscale child may possess all the materialistic things he or she desires, the lack of parental engagement is still problematic. Money doesn't raise children. The only difference between the communities is that the symptoms look different. For instance, Bloomberg confirmed that the perpetrators for the tragic pattern of mass school shootings are white, male, and socially isolated. This was based on a database compiled by *Mother Jones* that tracked ninety-eight mass shootings between 1982 and 2018.

The children we serve in schools run the full gamut of American communities. We served children with a myriad of traumatic experiences and unfortunate circumstances. It's imperative for us to provide necessary tools and resources to assist them. Instead of approaching curriculum from a privileged perspective, let's build it from an inclusive pathway.

Being intentional with engaging families around culture will help them show up as their authentic selves every time. Think about it, there isn't anyone on this planet who does not like to be celebrated. Most schools do a good job planning events for families, but very few plans are made with families. They normally come to spectate and support their children, which is a great thing, but opportunities are missed for richer interactions and dialogues. For example, during cultural events, a ton of time is spent researching information about various cultures for showcases and presentations. Imagine how powerful it would be if the caregivers were leveraged as the authentic research by sharing their upbringings, journeys, and family aspirations. That is a hack to empower parents, because their voices will be heard, and their children's self-identity will strengthen when they see their superheroes being valued.

One year, I had a student whose mom and dad agreed to participate in a Haitian Flag Day celebration at the school. They were both professional artists in the community. The mom performed folklore dance while the dad played African drums. The richness of that experience was etched within the entire school culture. Such an experience was beyond a form they could have filled out, a flyer sent home, or any of the other channels of communication we traditionally used to try to engage parents. As the visionary, it behooves you to consider discarding old ways of doing things and be open to innovative ideas that will create effective changes.

While it's vital for parents to feel seen and heard, it's equally important for their voices to be valued through implementation. Consequently, they will be more engaged and involved because they'll have a sense of safety and belonging. Can you imagine how powerful it would be if schools were to allow a parent representative in certain decision-making processes to help them create effective systems and procedures to better suit their respective student population? I'm sure the campuses that have tapped into parental resources are reaping enormous benefits. Is this a common practice at your school and/or district? If not, why? Since scholars come from diverse backgrounds, every school is unique, and every student learns differently, respective school culture and curriculum should be built on diversity. This will make way for equitable practices that bring meaning and context to learning in transformative ways. It is also a more effective way of building trust between students, teachers, and families.

## Community Involvement

In order to see education electrifying and alive, plug your curriculum into the community's resourceful outlet. Partnering with the community will give schools a power surge to provide better educational opportunities and outcomes for their students. Most of all, it will strengthen neighborhoods. As a result, increased engagement and involvement among families, businesses, and pertinent leaders will lead to a stronger, more invested community. In addition to academic assistance, there are local organizations that can support students who are struggling emotionally and socially. Principals, once you've nailed your robust curriculum, it's time to take it to the streets and leverage your neighboring allies.

If you don't seek and knock, doors will not open. As the leader of the school, consider leading the legwork by taking your leadership team and available teachers to canvas the school's neighborhood during the summer. I would strongly suggest securing funding to compensate your colleagues for their endeavors. Finding creative ways to incentivize the efforts is also a must. Walk into local businesses to spark conversations, dine at a nearby restaurant, inquire about collaboration, and converse with kids and families who are out in the community. Be sure to name your vision, your desire to get everyone involved, and specific next steps of engagement. By doing so, you can create a directory that will be readily available to plan the execution of your curriculum. Your interaction with caretakers of the students you're serving may give you insight on specific needs you weren't considering. This will enable you to embed impactful cultural opportunities for your students to experience deeper learning.

I'm aware that many districts have created school feeder patterns, where schools are designated for students to follow as they graduate from one level to the next. Since the schools are typically in the same neighborhoods, the goal is to keep the scholars together from elementary to high school. When administrators from the aforementioned campuses collaborate effectively, it's a win-win situation. Imagine adding the local community to that process as it pertains to resources, programs, and exposure opportunities.

Show me a neighborhood that has a strong school-community relationship, I'll guarantee you a thriving educational experience. When positive relationships are built among people, increased trust automatically follows. Understanding always resides where trust lives. Apply this truth to your school and the community it serves. I promise the benefits will trickle down to improved classroom management. Students behave better when they know and see a strong bond between their loved ones and educators. As a matter of fact, the mere presence of adults usually deters bad behavior. That is one of the reasons administrators ask their staff members to stand at their doors during class transitions.

I remember reading about a school in Louisiana that was experiencing volatile behavior and a high number of fights. A group of forty dads in the neighborhood decided to form an alliance called Dads on Duty, where they took shifts spending time at the school to greet students in the morning and help create a positive environment. The culture and vibe of the school changed as the fighting and police arrest decreased drastically. As reported, these men did not have degrees in counseling or criminal justice. They were concerned community leaders who wanted to help the young people in their neighborhoods. Consequently, the students felt safer, and the campus maintained a positive culture for learning.

I applaud the principal of that school and its leadership team for being open to the idea and congratulate the men for stepping up! This is a big deal! Fellas, trust me, educators will back me up on this: getting men to show up to school buildings is difficult. Yet, our presence is so vital for young people, it is transformative. This example is a drop in the bucket of the monumental impact a strong school–community relationship will have on education.

## Stakeholder's Think Tank

Have you ever called a meeting that reserved a seat at the table for every stakeholder who can impact the educational experience at your school? I'm talking about a parent representative, student body representative, local officials, clergy, business, and community-based organizations. This is one of the most powerful holistic approaches a school can adopt, because it will bring a range of resources and expertise to support students. I'm posing the question to challenge you as the leader on campus to harness the resources in your school's community into a unified ecosystem that will impact education in a variety of ways.

Bringing different stakeholders together will help increase communication and collaboration between them. As I mentioned before, relationships propel people to support ventures. Articulating your mission and vision to such a diverse group of people will ensure that everyone is on the same page regarding educational goals and priorities. Community leaders, organizations, and elected officials have a better understanding of the local needs and challenges faced by students and their families. By partnering with said individuals and entities, educators can gain valuable insights that can inform their teaching strategies and curriculum development. More importantly, the collaboration will lead to more effective decision-making.

Although teachers are one of the most underpaid and underappreciated professionals in the world, they tend to spend a significant amount of money and resources on their students. Between projects, trinkets, incentives, social needs, and other necessities that arise, educators do not hesitate to dig in their pockets to meet the needs of their pupils. Increasing access to funding and assistance will support educational initiatives that can include grants, donations, and volunteer manpower. Many people subscribe to the lofty notion that students deserve a high-quality and equitable education, but very few are willing to provide adequate backing to make it a reality. A tight unity with the local community stakeholders can assist the this situation.

Accountability is a word that is thrown around often but isn't always upheld. Very often, we tend to have good intentions, but it's not enough for sustainability. When stakeholders from different groups come together, they can hold each other accountable to assure that the needs and interests of all groups are being met. As a former assistant principal, I know firsthand how quickly we can get sidetracked by the daily obstacles and fires that demand our attention. Having a think tank of leaders to help pull us out of the weeds from time to time will serve as a safeguard to a fair and equitable system for all students.

If the focus is really on student outcomes, let's create processes that will prioritize them. Once the adults who have vested interest in student success commit to collaborate, it's vital to include students' input. Including a student representative in an educational stake-holder's meeting will ensure the perspectives and experiences of the primary beneficiaries of education are considered when decisions are being made.

Once the scholar is confident that students' voices are heard and valued, awareness will be promoted among their peers. This will increase valuable insights into what is and isn't working. They can share their plights, challenges, and suggestions for improvement, which can inform the decision-making process. After all, scholars are the ones who are impacted the most by the effects of the education system, so it makes sense to always keep in mind their best interest.

A community stakeholders meeting will increase involvement and improvement. The inclusivity will make community members feel invested in the success of local schools. This can lead to increased support for initiatives, as well as more effective partnerships between schools and local organizations. This is not a fly-by-night venture, but it is possible with intentionality and clear goals. By working together, a think tank of valued individuals will develop solutions to address a community's unique challenges and guarantee that all its students have access to a high-quality education.

## CHAPTER TAKEAWAYS

As the principal, you should put on your equity lens to create a curriculum that lives beyond the four walls of your campus and focuses on content that ignites deeper academic, social, and emotional learning.

- If you are going to hold families accountable for their children's education, you have to intentionally involve them in the educational process.
- Show me a neighborhood that has a strong school–community relationship, and I'll guarantee you a thriving educational experience.
- Seek to implement a think tank of school leaders, community stakeholders, and student representation to increase involvement and improvement.

## PROBE AND TRANSFORM

How are you aligning your school's curriculum with the student population and community you serve?

- How do you intentionally include students' voices in your decision-making processes?
- How have you leveraged parental engagement that goes beyond attending meetings, events, and discipline?

# EDUCATORS

As educators, you are in the business of continuous learning in order to liberate minds.

# Educator's Footprints

Educators' impact is so grand
Expert knowledge and patience at hand
In classrooms they shine
Guiding young mind divine
Tattooing footprints on futures unplanned.
They seek to ignite a creative spark
Crafting lessons like art to leave a mark
Teaching beyond books
They'd open new looks
Inquiring minds set to embark.
Through struggles and doubts they persist
Overworked and underpaid they insist
On shaping society
From a seed to fruitful tree
Uncommon resilience, none could resist.
Support educators to higher heights
When life's on stage they're the playwrights
With passion they strive
To keep minds alive
Guiding futures, shining their lights.

# 7 | EDUCATIONAL ROCK STAR

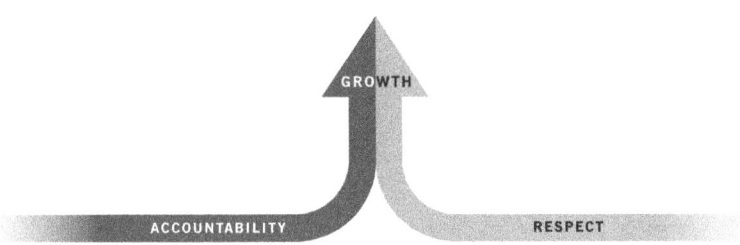

## *Respect* + Accountability = **Growth**

Educators, academic learning is fostered or failed inside the four walls of your classroom. The parents, administrators, and community stakeholders can all be on the same page, but if the classroom is not operating effectively, the work will be close to impossible. As educators, you are the nonnegotiable lifeline for the educational formula to be successful. You play a critical role in shaping the minds and character of the next generation. Better yet, educators have been molding society for generations. No matter who you are and what you do, you sat in a teacher's classroom to be able to function effectively.

No other profession has the capability nor honor to say they've had a hand in shaping the minds of every person on the planet. That's huge! I wish they would respect the profession and pay you as such, but that's another conversation for another time. It is essential for you as an educator to own the fact that you are the cornerstone of education, because of your ability to facilitate learning, help develop critical life skills, and serve as an added layer as a role model.

Being an educator is an inherently challenging and demanding profession, as supported by extensive research and real-world experiences. The constant juggling of heavy workloads, administrative pressures, emotional investment in students' behaviors and success, and the pressure to meet educational standards can lead to stress, burnout, and diminished job satisfaction among educators. To address these challenges and promote well-being, educators need to prioritize self-care. Practicing self-care is essential for maintaining their mental, emotional, and physical health.

Educators can engage in various self-care strategies to support their well-being. These strategies may include setting boundaries to protect personal time, engaging in relaxation techniques such as meditation, pursuing hobbies or activities outside of work, seeking social support from colleagues or support networks, and maintaining a healthy work–life balance. It is crucial to recognize that educators' self-care is not only beneficial for their own well-being but also for the overall educational ecosystem. When educators prioritize self-care, they can bring their best selves to the classroom, effectively support their students' learning and development, and contribute to a positive and nurturing educational environment.

Facilitating learning for three to four diverse groups of students with varying levels and personalities for a span of eight hours a day is hard work! Attending meetings, grading papers, preparing lesson plans, communicating with parents are among the myriad of responsibilities you carry on a daily basis. Being an educator is not for the faint of heart. From the bottom of my heart, I THANK YOU!

According to internationally acclaimed educator Jane Elliott, an educator is "One who is engaged in the act of leading people out of ignorance." In order to lead, one must know the way. As an educator, you are in the business of continuous learning in order to liberate minds. The information you deliver has to go beyond techniques to master standardized testing. This cannot be done if you're not fine-tuning your craft on a regular basis. The ultimate question is WHY are you an educator? It's important to answer that question with a genuine heart because it dictates every decision you will make both in and outside of the classroom.

I began my career in this profession as a substitute teacher. Back then, my "why" was to maintain something flexible that would supplement my income as a full-time entrepreneur. Working at a high school where the workday ended at 2:30 p.m. was perfect! Because the students responded to my leadership and high standards, the school's administration approached me on several occasions about teaching full-time. I respectfully declined, because I knew I was not willing to make the commitment at the time.

A few years later, circumstances changed, and I decided to entertain the offer. My "why" changed to giving back to schools in underserved communities by using my experiences to provide black male representation for students of color and give them an opportunity to receive an equitable education. That mindset gave me the laser focus to push past a plethora of challenges during my twenty-plus years as an educator.

If you are not in this field for the right reason, you will cause more damage than good. It will be educational injustice to the scholars who are placed under your leadership. If that's you, please politely exit stage left and transition into something that brings you fulfillment. Trust me, you'll be better for it, especially when it comes to your mental health. On the other hand, if you are in the education world for the right reasons, your "why" will be the right fit for a lot of young minds and communities.

Before we talk about the hard work you need to put in as you shape future generations, it is vital for you to maintain the practice of self-care. If you don't take care of yourself, you won't be equipped to meet the needs of your students. You must prioritize your well-being to be able to manage the stress and demands of the profession.

According to a student's article published in the *Journal of School Health*, teacher self-care practices were associated with lower levels of burnout, increased job satisfaction, and improved mental health (Hagenauer & Volet 2014). By demonstrating the importance of self-care, you'll also serve as a role model for your students to prioritize their own well-being and healthy habits.

I believe one of the most important components of an educator is to create a positive learning environment for students. Just like the principal needs to create a culture for the school, there has to be a healthy classroom culture as well. It's essential for relationship-building, engagement, and academic success. In addition, you have to set up routines and systems that provide stability, consistency, and fairness. Unfortunately, many novice educators drop the ball in this area and fall into the black hole of mismanaged classrooms. If you don't set standards and expectations for your scholars, they will set them up for you. Trust me, it will be disastrous on many levels.

School leaders should prioritize supporting newbies with tools, strategies, and mentor educators who have been through the trenches. Children thrive when they're in a disciplined, supportive, and safe space. This is especially true for immigrant students in your classrooms who face the daunting task of learning a new language and adapting to a new culture.

It has been over thirty years since I migrated from Haiti to Little Haiti in Miami. I still remember the names of my two English language learner (ELL) teachers. Mr. Ellis and Ms. Rawlings were angels from heaven, as far as I was concerned. In addition to the culture shock, Haitian students were targeted with derogatory insults, harassed, and beaten for no reason. As a matter of fact, a lot of children of Haitian descent denounced their heritage and claimed to be Jamaican, Bahamian, or any other culture but Haitian. The walk to and from school felt like a war zone, but my ELL teachers were allies who provided support and some solace during the school day. They checked in on me before, after, and during class. They made me feel safe to communicate orally and in writing in my native language. They made me feel like I mattered, which motivated me to push past the obstacles I was facing. With their assistance, I was able to display the academic skills I learned in my country.

A year later, I was placed in advanced classes. The level of trust was critical in fostering a learning environment that enabled me to succeed. Another layer to my growth was the seamless unity between my two angels and my content educators. If they didn't get along, they did a great job hiding it from the student body.

There has to be a positive and efficient relationship with support staff, whether it's ELL, Exceptional Student Education (ESE), or paraprofessionals. The stronger the adults work to build a healthy learning community, the greater the accountability, and, most importantly, the more students will grow.

You can't teach what you don't know. Proper training is crucial for you as an educator to develop the necessary knowledge, skills, and competencies to deliver effective instructions and create a positive learning environment for your students. This groundwork ensures that educators understand legal and ethical obligations to education. This includes, but is not limited to, laws, regulations, child welfare, and privacy. Teachers without formal college training in education have a bigger learning curve, because it's a lot to learn and figure out in the midst of adapting to multiple moving pieces.

Regardless of your background, I strongly encourage all educators to engage in ongoing professional development to stay up-to-date with the latest research, technologies, and best practices in the field. An effective part of that training is the ability to leverage the expertise of your colleagues. Get into the habit of observing one another for successful strategies and collaborating on projects.

Having studied engineering in college, I knew nothing about pedagogy. During my years as a substitute, I asked seasoned educators questions about the craft and observed some of their practices. When I transitioned to being a full-timer, I had the privilege of working alongside some of the best educators on the planet. Of course, I attended the professional development for certification, but the crew at the View (Lakeview Elementary in Miami) helped build my skill set to levels way beyond my capacity. My competitive edge and eagerness to learn pushed me to be an avid student, but most importantly, the team built my capacity. After a few years, I earned Rookie Teacher of The Year, and I never looked back.

We worked so well as a family, we took a small, no name, and underserved community school from an F to a AAA powerhouse. Giving a school a grade based on standardized state testing results is not my cup of tea, but I had to throw that accomplishment in there because we saw the growth in the students, staff, and the community.

As an educator, you have to know your end goal at the beginning. Similar to lesson planning, use the product and plan backwards. I knew I didn't want to stay in the classroom for my entire career. I made sure I learned as much as I could, took advantage of leadership opportunities, and stayed ready when doors opened for me. My transition as a reading coach happened at a different school in a different district where I didn't know anyone. My training gave me the right to be confident in my abilities to do the job well.

After two years, I was offered an assistant principal position to further my career. Those things didn't happen haphazardly. I was intentional about becoming a highly effective educator. I supported student growth on every level to enhance learning outcomes. I managed my classrooms, and engaged in ongoing development. To be honest, I was not pursuing an assistant principal position. I was offered the position based on my track record and work ethics. When the opening became available, I was considered. The lesson learned in that situation is: your work will speak for you. Your standards and productivity will script the narrative.

## Fluid Data

Education in America has become a numbers game. It's more about economics than education. Poli-tricks, bureaucracies, and lobbyists are some of the major sharks that are devouring the life of society's future. It seems like the more casualties, the more ferocious they become. They leave their consciences in parking lots before entering board rooms to pass legislation and bills that ultimately become multimillion-dollar bills in their bank accounts, at the expense of marginalized and impoverished communities. Did I mention that public schooling in these "United"

States is still functioning on the foundation of biased educational bylaws that were adopted since the 1800s?

Now that we got that out of the way, let's shift our focus back to the fleeting data. States are holding school districts in deadly choke holds to produce "passing scores" on standardized testing. Districts shift the pressure to principals, who in turn inject educators with anxiety syringes to manufacture test dummies. Instead of educating children, most educators find themselves succumbing to the strained squeeze. Additionally, the trend of increased class sizes makes productivity almost impossible. The last time I checked, an overpopulated classroom is a guaranteed formula for declining quality of education and rise in complex social problems. If these things don't sound emergency threat alarms for a country, I don't know what will.

Focusing on the locus of your control is the best way to survive the educational landscape. While the government, districts, and administrators analyze their data to rate your effectiveness as an educator, you should use a combination of other pertinent data points to develop a comprehensive picture of your impact. By doing so, you will maintain your sanity, focus on children and families, and fan the flicker of joy in your soul.

Let us make school engaging again. Students should be the main characters in the plot instead of minor characters who vanish in tragic crossfires. Create a positive learning environment they consider "fun" that will give them an incentive to want to show up to your classes, thereby raising attendance percentage. Naturally, parents and community members will catch wind of your awesomeness, because the children will be your mouthpiece. When kids are in their parents' ears about something they enjoy, there is no stopping their relentless energy. As a result, guardians will be satisfied and eager to collaborate. This approach is more than tracking test scores. Honestly, it's better! Having read that statement, some administrators may think this is not a chapter they'd want their staff to read, but nothing could be further from the truth.

Instead of spotlighting student achievement on standardized tests, zoom in on student growth. At the beginning of the year, create student folders, have the scholars document their baseline data, and have them track their progress as it pertains to grades and assessments. While some scholars are working at grade level, there are some in the same classroom who are years away from reaching that capacity. At the end of the day, they all can learn. Our job as educators is to create a pathway to success to make them experience self-efficacy, to see connections between their initial baseline and progressive learning.

Educating students at different levels and learning styles requires different processes, content, and products. Your mindset as an educator has to be one who is constantly engaged in innovative practices that support learning and value the population you serve. Again, the primary pillar is social relationships with students and the community. Second, you have to present information to scholars in a way that helps them process and connect with it, whether it's culturally, socially, or emotionally.

One of the best and simplest ways to gather this data is to have students fill out information on Google Forms about their interests, cultures, and experiences. As you plan your units, glance at that data to help you differentiate and create relevant products to show what they learned.

One of the best strategies to meet students where they are while providing support as they learn new concepts and skills is called scaffolding. As an educator, you are constantly assessing students' prior knowledge and understanding of the subject matter. This will help you to determine what support is needed. It doesn't make sense to assign a five-paragraph essay for your entire class when you have scholars who can barely write one paragraph. You have to break down the learning objective into smaller, manageable parts to help students develop a deeper understanding of the subject matter and become more confident learners.

The key is to provide clear instructions and expectations. Make sure they understand what they're supposed to do and how they will be assessed, preferably using a rubric. Utilize the data you gathered from the Google Forms, your classroom observations, and other pertinent information to engage students in the learning process. This could include visuals aids, hands-on activities, or well-crafted productive group work.

One year, I taught writing courses that included sections of middle school boys. Once I noticed the zeal for football, we worked on an argument essay about whether or not it was safe to play tackle football. You can imagine their initial reaction to the controversial prompt. They were eager to prove me wrong. They analyzed research in order to support their positions. It was fulfilling to read some of their responses after they learned the debilitating health factors associated with the sport. Needless to say, I didn't have any issues with engagement, because I intentionally chose a topic they enjoyed.

Another important aspect of scaffolding, or good teaching, is modeling. You have to show students how to complete tasks or solve problems. This will help students see what is expected and how to apply the knowledge or skill they are learning. As they begin to practice the steps on their own, you must provide feedback and guidance throughout the process in order to identify areas of improvement and make effective adjustments. Eventually, you should gradually remove support as students become more confident and independent in their learning.

Notice, I haven't mentioned anything about teaching to a standardized test. Scholars need to acquire critical thinking skills to navigate education and life beyond the classroom. Once they're equipped, they will succeed!

I remember at one point my reading students were banned from saying "FCAT" (Florida Comprehensive Assessment Test) in my classroom. At the time, it was the annual standardized achievement exam students in grades three through ten had to take in the state of Florida. It was like a curse word in my space. I had them buy into the fact that, as long as they came to school and gave me their best, I would make sure they learned the skills to pass any test put in front of them. I familiarized myself with the standards and used my creativity to deliver the lessons. I took some of the boring reading passages in the outdated reading book we had to use and turned them into short plays.

The caveat was that, in order to participate in the skits, they had to pay close attention during the audio read aloud, classroom discussion, and take good notes. In doing so, they became familiar with the characters and understood the plot. We had a blast! One time, the principal heard the commotion, walked in the room with a concerned look, and asked why they weren't reading silently. By the time she left, the students were able to break down the story and academic content in their own unique ways. She silently exited stage left. Year after year, I delivered, and they passed the reading comprehension test. I didn't do anything magical. I simply taught the content to my students' interests and learning profiles.

Teaching pedagogy, metacognitive skills, academic language, and other educational strategies to effectively engage students is not a fly-by-night process. They are high-functioning tools you can only master through professional development training and proper practice. The same way students are expected to experience and manipulate information until mastery is the same process for you as an educator. If you teach multiple sections of a subject area, teach a rigorous and complex differentiated lesson to all your classes, despite varying levels. When I was in the classroom, I had an enrichment folder that contained challenging tasks that students were able to complete when they were done with their classwork. Typically, those kinds of assignments were usually reserved for "gifted" scholars, but I challenged every one of my students to engage with at least one of those activities during each semester. I was amazed at the products my lower-level students were able to produce. Students will rise to the standard you set for them.

## CHAPTER TAKEAWAYS

Teaching is the only profession that has the capability and honor to say it has had a hand in shaping the minds of every person on the planet.

- As an educator, you are in the business of continuous learning in order to liberate minds. Your training will give you the right to be confident in your abilities to do the job well.
- Instead of spotlighting student achievement on standardized tests, zoom in on student growth.
- Present information to scholars in a way that helps them process and connect with it culturally, socially, or emotionally.

## PROBE AND TRANSFORM

How are you actively seeking to build your capacity as an educator?

- How are you making sure to include self-care as part of your routine?
- How do you build relationships with your students?
- How do you use those data points in your planning?

## Leave No Mind Behind

Let's burn the traditional ways of education
Transition into hands-on learning
A pathway that leaves no mind behind
A boundless world with tactile might
That sculpt scholars from spectators
To creators and innovators
Living out curiosity's dreams
Unleashing wonders, touching the unseen.
Embracing the impossible while witnessing miracles
Every field, in every art
Hands-on learning plays a big part
Through action and practice, knowledge is won
Perspectives evolve, boundaries rearranged
Senses engaged, passions ignite
With minds and bodies intertwined in unity
Learning transcends what textbooks suggest
The world is the classroom
Experience is the teacher
Together they create a path
That leaves no mind behind.

# 8 | BEYOND THE CLASSROOM WALLS

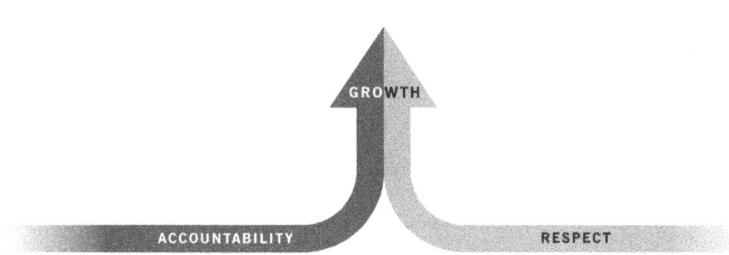

## *Respect* **+ Accountability = Growth**

It's been proven that we retain a little more than 20 percent of information we learn in school. On the other hand, we have a 75 percent retention rate when we experience learning through hands-on practice. As a product of the educational system in America, I can attest to the fact that the overall processes of education are a major disservice to students. While there are silos of schools and individuals who are effectively educating children, the overall system is not adequately preparing scholars for college, careers, and real life. Because today's students are graduating in a rapidly changing world, our practices should continuously adjust as well. In order to help them see the relevance and practical applications of what they are learning, we have to give them access to experiential learning beyond the classroom walls.

## Project-Based Learning

One of the most common practices schools use to engage students is project-based learning (PBL). It is inherently effective because it requires students to work on a project that is personally meaningful to them and their communities. This increases motivation and interest in the subject matter, which ultimately promotes a deeper understanding of the material. PBL allows students to apply what they've learned in school in real-world situations. It often involves collaborative group work that fosters communication and teamwork skills. These skills are essential in their academic and professional careers. Moreover, PBL requires students to be creative, think critically, self-reflect, inquire, and solve problems. Lastly, it allows them to take ownership of their learning and work independently to achieve goals. This is essential for self-directed practices for them to become independent learners.

Incorporating PBL into the curriculum requires cohesiveness from administrators, staff, and sometimes the community. Otherwise, it is impossible. As the educator in the classroom, it behooves you to take a look at your School Improvement Plan (SIP) to see how it's aligned with the curriculum. If possible, reach out to students, parents, and neighboring leaders to inquire about their top three to five problems they'd like to solve in the local community. It's vital to recruit community partners who represent the racial and cultural diversity of your school population. If you have a content area coach, sit down with him or her to identify the learning strands for each semester.

As a team, align all this information to choose a relevant topic and learning objectives. Define what you want students to learn and how you will know whether they've learned it. Next, collaborate with other content area educators to work smarter and not harder. Plan the project by breaking it down into manageable steps and setting clear expectations for student participation and deliverables. This should include roles and responsibilities for each team member, setting deadlines for completion, and outlining the final product or presentation.

Previously, I spoke about the need for scaffolding. It's a support that is definitely necessary in this situation for all students, including ELLs and those with special needs. Most of all, evaluating student learning should be an equitable process that assesses their final product, presentation, and participation with rubrics, peer evaluation, and self-assessments. As I mentioned before, this is not something you should do alone. Additionally, there's no need to re-create the wheel because there are tons of projects and resources that have already been created and can be tweaked to fit your needs. Get inspired by the project ideas at PBL Works (pblworks.org) and at EL Education's Models of Excellence. (https://modelsofexcellence.eleducation.org/).

Overall, PBLs are effective because they challenge students intellectually by inviting them to answer meaningful and complex questions. They also propel scholars to work in a team to learn empathy, interdependence, and accountability. On a school level, PBLs force administration to provide training, support, and professional development time to collaborate and plan for successful projects. To take it a step further, it would be extremely beneficial to leverage a planning day to engage teachers as learners in a proposed project so they get a chance to immerse themselves in the process and work out any kinks they may find.

## Service-Learning Projects

No matter how advanced technology becomes, it will never be able to replace the human experience. Social media, artificial intelligence, and other innovative tools are great in their own respects, but they are also disengaging people from authentic participation. In addition to academic learning, service-learning projects provide scholars with civic engagement, real-world experience, personal growth, and career exploration.

Phones and tablets have turned students into zombies. Their eyes and minds are glued to a myriad of unsolicited and inappropriate online information. As a result, we've become a society that would rather record an act of violence instead of helping to save someone's life. Service-learning projects can help humanize life and provide opportunities for students to engage in meaningful activities. This can assist with a sense of responsibility and commitment to their community. Additionally, they will cultivate a sense of empathy and compassion for others.

For instance, working with individuals or groups who are less fortunate, young people can gain a better understanding of social issues and obtain a deeper appreciation for the diverse needs and experiences of others. Moreover, service-learning projects can expose scholars to different career paths and explore potential career interests, which is particularly valuable for those who are unsure about their future career plans.

Similar to PBL, service-learning projects should not be done in isolation. They should be aligned with learning objectives and implemented with a schoolwide approach. Based on the content area, educators may choose to involve pertinent local organizations or community groups to identify a project that meets the needs of both the students and the community. As a society, we don't have to look far to identify needs. In every corner in every neighborhood, in every city, there are a myriad of issues that need a transformative touch. Once they're made known, there should be a collective effort to provide solutions that will engage the youth to give them a greater sense of social responsibility.

Lastly, research has shown that students who participate in service-learning projects have higher levels of academic achievement.

Having the opportunity to turn theoretical learning into hands-on experiences enables scholars to use critical thinking skills. This sort of engagement motivates them to want to show up physically and mentally. It also helps students better understand the relevance of what they are learning. The more interaction they have with the world around them, the more they're developing communication skills that are essential for academic success, such as effective writing, speaking, and listening skills. As an educator, if you subscribe to the fact that your job is to equip students with the skills and knowledge they need to become responsible and engaged members of their community, service-learning projects are essential.

## Field Trips

Another component of experiential learning is the use of field trips. They provide students with exposure to different experiences, cultures, and environments they may not have access to otherwise. As a result, their understanding of the world is enriched, and their perspectives are broadened.

I remember being on a field trip with a group of fifth graders to watch a production at a local theater in Miami. I was sitting next to a young man who told me that was his first time on the highway (Interstate 95) and at a theater. I was surprised, because I would've never guessed that a ten-year-old child living in an urban city like Miami would have been deprived of what I considered to be a basic excursion. At the end of that day, we strengthened our relationship and were able to connect on a deeper level. It is vital for you as an educator to break the monotony of routine classroom activities and offer your scholars a chance to learn in a new and exciting environment. Such opportunities will create meaningful learning opportunities and memories for you, and your students, that can last a lifetime.

## Technology-Based learning

Technology-based learning, also known as e-learning, is becoming increasingly important for students. Although unregulated technology use can be detrimental, the lack of it will produce the same result. We are living in an era where information and innovation are at an all-time high. Resources for school and everyday life are being transferred into digital platforms. As society evolves, the way education is presented has to adapt as well in order to give our scholars access to success. Some of the supplemental resources that can be utilized for lesson planning should include videos, podcasts, online libraries, and interactive simulations, to name a few.

Teaching mainstream classes that include students with varying levels of comprehension is more of a reason for you to use tools that will give you flexibility and customization. Truth be told, the majority of educators don't have the luxury of special education and support staff in their classroom to assist with scholars who require special accommodations. Technology-based learning can be beneficial by allowing students to work at their own pace. Certain resources can be customized to meet the individual needs of students by providing different levels of content, assessments, and feedback based on their progress. I'm not condoning the practice of putting a child on a computer program as the primary means of education. Unfortunately, this has become a practice for some ineffective educators who either do not want to deal with certain students or don't have the skill set to deliver the academic content. Either way, I implore you to ask for help: partner up with your support staff (ESE, ESOL, paraprofessionals, content coaches). Leverage the manpower and technology you have at your disposal to give scholars the equitable education they deserve.

The future is now. You cannot educate children with the exact same tools that were used when you were a student. Yes, there are some fundamental strategies that are still effective, but technology has become a major player in academics and professional endeavors. Despite the obvious, many school districts tolerate the disparity of not equipping all schools with the same resources. The sad truth is many students are excluded from access due to disability, socioeconomic status, or geographic location. As the educator in the classroom, you should make it a priority to ensure that equity and diversity exist in your space on all levels. Inclusive technology-based learning can spark innovation by encouraging scholars from diverse backgrounds to bring their unique ideas and perspectives to the table. Thus, providing the future-readiness students need to succeed in a rapidly changing world.

## Internships

Internships are game changers! Connecting classroom learning with the working world is the biggest liberation an educator can provide to students. It unlocks possibilities beyond the school walls. It is imperative that all students—not just the ones with the best grades or connections—are granted the opportunity to participate in meaningful internships. In addition to hands-on learning, they allow scholars to explore different career paths and industries, which will help them make informed decisions about their future.

In order to maximize internships, they have to be planned and student centered. An inventory of each scholar's interest should drive the internship experience. From there, educators can possibly create a semester theme or essential question that students can investigate with experts from their work sites. At that point, targeted community organizations can be contacted to make the connections. Prior to the start of this great experience, clear learning goals and expectations should be established among students, work sites, and school to facilitate meaningful outcomes for all parties involved. Although internships typically begin in high school, I believe middle school should be the starting point. They don't have to be long to provide the necessary experience. Collaborating with guardians can help facilitate a mentor-shadowing process during the many breaks and holidays throughout the school year.

"How will this schoolwork benefit me in life?" This is the question we hear more often than not from students. As a matter of fact, it's a question I used to ask on numerous occasions when I was in school. Research and experience have taught us that young people need more than academics to be prepared for life. There is a plethora of essential competencies like decision-making, time management, social skills, and cultural nuances that can be learned away from campuses. Making these practical connections accessible by partnering with local schools is one of the most powerful opportunities you can provide to students.

While educators can provide the foundation for subject matter, local professionals can assist in engaging students in hands-on learning that will exponentially enhance their learning capacities. Furthermore, they allow scholars to pinpoint, explore, and pursue their passions. This is vital, because studies show that the majority of people in the workplace are not satisfied with their jobs or careers. They show up because they have bills to pay. Early exposure to the workforce will afford students the opportunity to learn job-specific skills, how to communicate with adults in a non-school setting, and newfound motivation.

I had the honor of spending a day with a banker when I was in high school. At the time, I knew I wanted to do something along the lines of business but had no knowledge of business itself. The gentleman was very cool and approachable. He took me around to his meetings and day-to-day activities. By the time the day was through, I was over the banking industry. Although it wasn't a bad experience, I realized that I wasn't excited about that type of work. It was eye-opening, because in my young limited mind, I anticipated a more fulfilling outcome.

On the other hand, my outlook on the banking industry could've been different if I had a chance to reflect and engage in deeper conversations with the mentor. Knowing what I know now about the various aspects of business, I'm confident I didn't get a chance to see a comprehensive view of the career. If the interaction was more structured and intentional, we could have taken a deeper dive into business options. This goes to show that clear communication and learning goals are essential between students, work sites, and schools in order to provide a meaningful project. Mentors have to be aware of the scope of work, and equipped with effective techniques to guide the process from beginning to end. At that point, they can debrief with scholars about their learning and growth, as the students link the learning partnership with academic content and personal interest.

At the end of a great internship experience, students should have a reflection meeting to discuss with their teacher and mentor. It is a necessary space to identify learning growth and foster an ongoing partnership. Scholars will become motivated, because they'll be able to see the relevance of school curriculum, accountability, and responsibility to turn in work on time. More importantly, they will have an increased awareness of what they want to do after graduation, whether it's college, technical school, or entrepreneurship. As the classroom educator, you have the ability to give them access to obtain a passport to those destinations.

## CHAPTER TAKEAWAYS

Scholars are graduating in a rapidly changing world. Our practices should continuously adjust as well.

- Project-based learning propels students to work in a team to learn empathy, interdependence, accountability, think critically, and ultimately become dependent learners.
- Technology will never be able to replace the human experience. Service-learning projects provide scholars with civic engagement, real-world experience, personal growth, and career exploration.
- Field trips provide students with exposure to different experiences, cultures, and environments they may not have access to otherwise.
- Connecting classroom learning with the working world is the biggest liberation an educator can provide to students.

## PROBE AND TRANSFORM

How do you incorporate real-world examples and applications into your teaching?

- How do you integrate technology and digital literacy skills into your curriculum to prepare students for the digital age?
- How are you creating opportunities to provide students with exposure to different career paths and the world of work?
- How do you incorporate financial literacy and practical life skills into your teaching?
- Can you describe any specific projects or initiatives that have connected your students with real-world problems and solutions?

# COMMUNITY LEADERS

While schools are responsible for educating young minds, community organizations work towards shaping their future and improving the quality of life for their local neighborhoods.

# A World to Share

Imagine a symphony, harmonious and bold
Where classroom and community unfold
Like a dance, stepping to a rhythm in sync
A collaboration profound, as destinies link.
Marvel at the mentor, guiding a child's way
Supporting dreams, lighting the pathway
Together they soar, on dream's gentle breeze
School and organization, empowering with ease.
Skilled like an athlete, passion aflame
Training and discipline, purpose beyond fame
Guided by coaches and leaders to overcome fear
School and organization, making futures clear.
When minds unite, passions align
Bridges flourish, results are divine
The gifts of knowledge, support, and care
School and organization, a world to share.

# 9 | COMMUNITY VITALIZATION

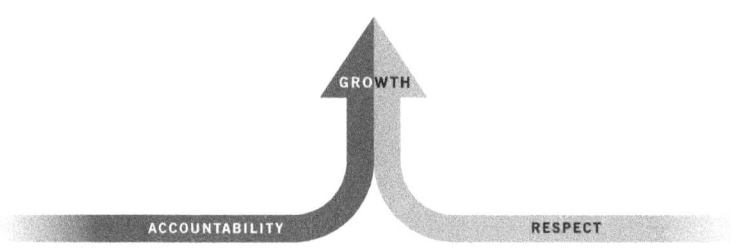

## *Respect* + Accountability = **Growth**

As a community organization, you are essential to the vitality and development of your city. While schools are responsible for educating young minds, community organizations work towards shaping their future and improving the quality of life for their local neighborhoods. Your engagement with local schools will enhance the youth's education in various ways. It will increase the visibility and understanding of issues around them and empower them to partake in decisions that affect their cities and everyday lives.

Adequate school funding is a detrimental disparity in schools in the United States and other parts of the world. As a result, local organizations are in positions to help fill the unfortunate gaps by supporting schools in several ways. More often than not, schools in low-income communities struggle with obtaining textbooks, access to technology, equipment, and resources for extracurricular activities. As much as some school leaders may want to provide better learning environments for students to enhance the quality of education, some of their hands are tied due to limited funding. Whether you choose to donate from the kindness of your heart or as a tax-deductible gift, I want you to know that a vast number of local schools need your assistance.

In the twenty-plus years I spent working in the school system, I've seen a steady decline in manpower and talent. Brain drain in the field of education is a real crisis, leaving school staff overworked and exhausted. Oftentimes, people are quicker to be critical before offering a solution or putting a hand to the plow. In addition to funds, organizations can also offer volunteers to work in schools as mentors, tutors, and coaches. This can provide students and educators support, encouragement, and guidance to help them succeed academically, professionally, and socially.

Additionally, local organizations can help families advocate for a richer and equitable education for their children. Educational workshops can be arranged where families learn about their rights and guidance on how to navigate the system. This is crucial for immigrant parents who are new to this country. A study published in the *Journal of Educational and Psychological Consultation* found that partnerships between community organizations and legal-service providers were instrumental in helping families navigate special education processes and advocate for their children's rights. Although technology has closed the gap with translation services, it is still imperative for local officials and organizations to assist by facilitating collaboration and networking among families, fostering a sense of community and shared purpose. They can provide training and capacity-building programs for families to enhance their advocacy skills. These pieces of evidence underscore the importance of local organizations in supporting families' advocacy efforts for better education.

Cultural awareness is a huge barrier for many people who are new to America. There are many civic and nonprofit organizations, but very few provide cultural awareness training to school staff to help them better understand the unique needs and experiences of immigrant families. It's a privilege for me to be in a position to consult in this area for the Haitian community. I've spoken to parents who refuse to come to schools because they're afraid of humiliation and deportation. Others are not privy to resources in their home languages that can help them and their children.

Quite frankly, a lot of cultural training and access can be done in congregations and community centers. The National Education

Association emphasizes the importance of professional development in cultural competency, stating that it enhances educators' ability to create supportive and equitable learning environments. This will help them develop a deeper understanding of diverse cultures and promote inclusive practices. Local organizations, such as public libraries or cultural heritage organizations, can collaborate with schools to curate culturally diverse collections, performances, exhibitions, cultural arts, and offer guidance on integrating these resources into the curriculum. Through training, resource sharing, community engagement, and partnerships for cultural programming, these organizations help schools create inclusive environments where students can develop cultural competence, empathy, and respect for diverse cultures.

## Internship

Our future leaders being able to pursue a real-world interest prior to college and having the opportunity to change their minds before they spend thousands of dollars on a major they will not enjoy as a career is powerful. Truth be told, there are countless college graduates who are working in fields they did not study during their collegiate years.

I'm a living testament of the said dilemma. I have two degrees in engineering that I haven't used in decades. I was so focused on sports that I chose my major on the strength of having a backup plan that made a lot of money. It wasn't a bad idea, but I needed wiser guidance. When my backup plan became the primary option, I was miserable. The money wasn't enough to keep me suited up in a corporate office doing engineering work. As an expert in your field, this is an area you can support schools in as they seek to provide structures to make these life-changing opportunities accessible to all scholars, not just the ones with high grade point averages.

Whether you're an entrepreneur, working in corporate America, on a college campus, vocational school, and some other place of business, you are in a prime position to help tailor meaningful experiences that students can use to gain deeper knowledge and guidance to make passionate decisions for their lives after high school graduation.

Your business will benefit in several ways when you open your doors to provide mentorships and internships for students. Those opportunities will help you identify talented individuals who may be a good fit for your organization. Recruitment is a component that keeps businesses competitive. If I may add, this will also help you save money. By working closely with students, you can evaluate their skills, work habits, and potential for future employment.

Another asset to partnering with schools is improved productivity. The students will bring fresh perspective and new ideas to the workplace. As you are aware, innovation is an element that makes your company stand out and is relevant to your customers and the culture you're serving. Furthermore, they can take on tasks that may otherwise be neglected, freeing employees to focus on higher-level projects. This is crucial to your ability to keep your workforce from being overworked and stressed. To take it a step further, as students build their skills at your place of business, this can lead to increased job satisfaction and loyalty to the company. This is a formula that can improve retention rates for your business as well as schools.

Professional exposure outside of school can serve as motivation and accountability for students. Imagine how enthused high school students would be to work in classrooms three days a week and spend two days engaged in a real-world setting. Not only will their background experiences expand, they will also broaden their networks. The same can be true for middle school students who can complete volunteer hours on the weekends or scheduled time on holidays and breaks. These important connections will truly aid scholars with a keen awareness of what they want to do after graduation. Not to mention the value it adds to your company in terms of good reputation and visibility. Studies have found that internships enhance equity, rigor, and school culture. This is definitely a win-win situation for businesses and schools and needs to be a staple in every community.

Networking is the hack for advancement in any field. The quicker this skill is learned, the further it will take an individual. Internships are primed to give students the opportunity to connect with people in their field of interest. In addition to gaining valuable insights and advice from experienced professionals, they will also build relationships. Such exposure will expand their network and learn about careers they probably wouldn't think of. If they perform well during their internships, they may be able to secure recommendations, referrals, or future employment opportunities.

Skill development is another vital component of internships. Companies are continuously investing in the latest technologies and tools to be competitive in their markets. Interns usually have access to these tools, which are less likely to be on their school's campus. As a result, they can develop new technical skills, knowledge of industry trends, and learn best practices along the way. As mentors provide feedback and guidance on their work, they improve their performance. Most of the time, company projects are done with team collaboration, which is a skill students should be learning in school. It can be fine-tuned in an internship setting. They'll have no choice but to work on their communication skills and learn how to express themselves in a professional setting.

Lastly, internships will help with time management and organization skills. Interns are often assigned tasks with specific deadlines. When working with a company, they will understand the value of why people say time is money.

Nothing is more deflating for college graduates than to finally obtain their degrees and be told they're not fully qualified for lack of job experience. I know I went through my share of rejection letters, and it was disheartening. As a business entity, you can set the next generation up for success by utilizing internships to build their résumés at an early age. They can attain relevant work experience in a specific field of study and demonstrate their skills and abilities to potential employers. This will make them well-rounded and attractive candidates. Not to mention the opportunity to work on projects or initiatives that result in tangible accomplishments that can be highlighted on a résumé. The experiences gained through an internship can help students with college acceptance, job search skills, résumé writing, interviewing, and access to professional references.

The more positive adults who come alongside students to support their educational journeys, the higher their chances that the student will succeed. As a result, strong lifelong relationships will be built between the youth and trusted adults in the community. Families will ultimately create bonds and trust within the educational village. Lastly, a boost in businesses and the local economy will organically follow, because parents will more than likely support the people who are supporting their children. Success is intertwined with these vital connections. Communal cohesion will have a direct impact on academic success. Trusted local leaders will be able to help parents and teachers with an additional strand of accountability for scholars. Moreover, our young people will have a higher level of respect for themselves, adults, and businesses in their communities. In the end, everyone wins!

## CHAPTER TAKEAWAYS

Organizations can offer volunteers to work in schools as mentors, tutors, and coaches.

- Local organizations can help families advocate for a richer and equitable education for their children.
- Provide life-changing internship opportunities to all scholars, not just the ones with high grade point averages.
- As a business entity, you can set the next generation up for success by utilizing internships to build their capacities and résumés at an early age.
- Internships are beneficial for both the students and the organizations.

## PROBE AND TRANSFORM

How do local organizations collaborate with the schools to support children's education in your neighborhood?

- How does the school in your area and the local organizations jointly address and support the diverse cultural, social, and emotional needs of children?
- What strategies or mechanisms are in place to ensure ongoing communication, coordination, and alignment between the school and the local organization in supporting children's education?

# STUDENTS

There are people around YOU who are working hard to make sure YOU succeed. None of their efforts matter if YOU don't work hard to make sure success happens.

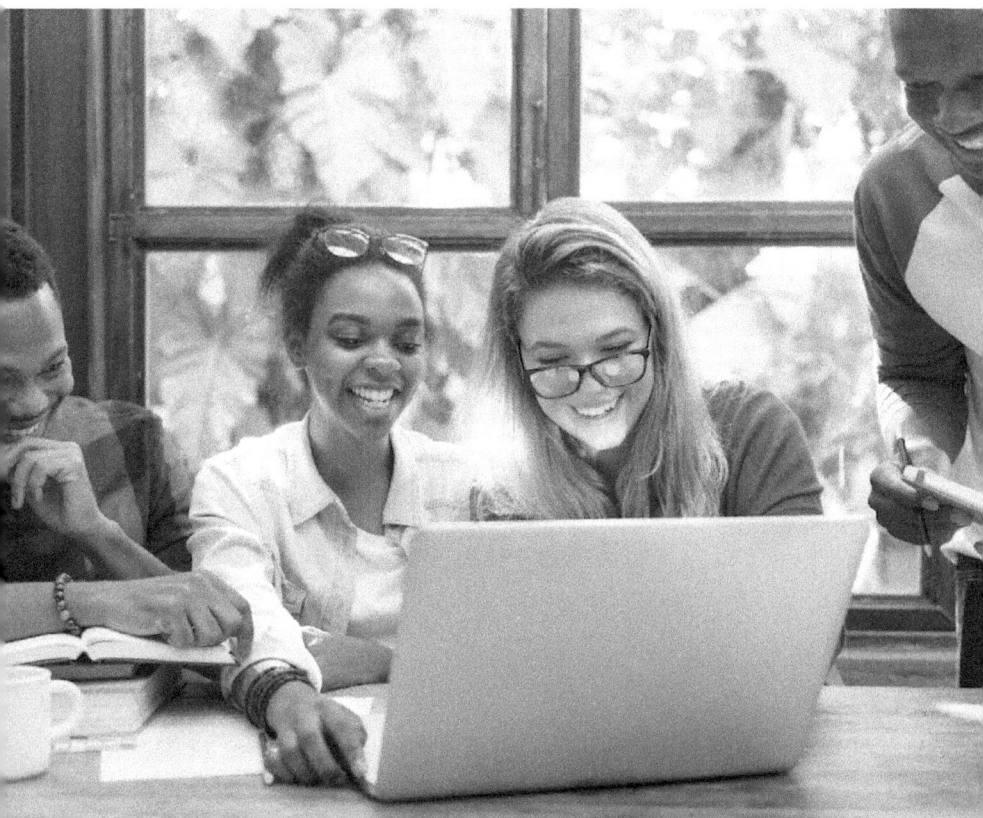

# Own Your Education

In the tapestry of education

You are the weaver and the thread

Shaping the fabric of your own learning

Own your education with fierce determination

It's a privilege that can never be taken for granted.

Your life is a canvas waiting to be painted

With colors of your dreams and aspirations

You hold the paintbrush

The adults who support you will provide the tools.

Along your journey, there are beacons of light

Mentors, educators, leaders, classmates

Who stand beside you with wisdom and support

To illuminate your path and ignite your curiosity.

With gratitude, honor the extraordinary individuals

Who selflessly dedicate their lives to help shape
your growth

Their impact extends beyond the classroom

Reaching deep into the fibers of your being.

In the tapestry of education

You are the weaver and the thread

Shaping the fabric of your own learning

Own your education with fierce determination

It's a privilege that can never be taken for granted

# 10 | OWN YOUR EDUCATION

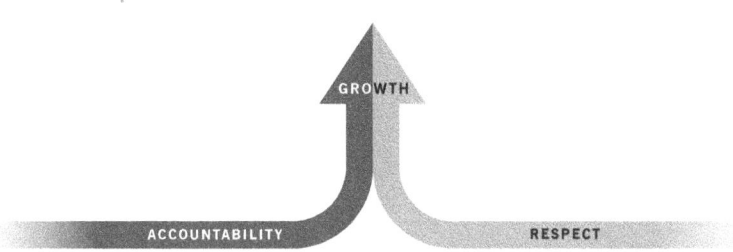

## *Respect* + Accountability = **Growth**

The first nine chapters of this book outline the sea of people who diligently work to make sure you receive a fundamental human right called education. If you are blessed to be in a position where you are receiving a free education, you should be grateful because there are many children around the world who do not have the same kind of access or whose guardians have to pay a fee for it. There are people around YOU who are working hard to make sure YOU succeed, none of their efforts matter if YOU don't work hard to make sure success happens.

Every morning, thousands of individuals wake up to drive cars and buses, clean schools, prepare meals, stand at crosswalks, prepare lesson plans, secure buildings, lose sleep, spend money, sacrifice time, and leave their families to invest in YOUR future. Let that sink in for a minute. I'll take it a step further by reminding you that many people have died to give you the opportunity to have access to education. Although education is a human right, historically that right hasn't always been given freely to everyone. In America, black and brown people were denied education for centuries, a litany of our ancestors lost their lives fighting for it. If you are a black or brown student reading this, I want you to know that you should honor and respect the sweat, blood, and tears of those who came before you who made it possible. It is not acceptable for you to waste all of those sacrifices. It would be ungrateful of you to not acknowledge these efforts. Truth has a way of liberating. I'm taking the liberty to inform you that parents are overwhelmed, administrators are frustrated, and teachers are burned out and leaving the profession because of YOU. Yes, you! It may not be you as an individual because you're doing the right thing, but the word, YOU, can represent the overall student body. Whether you're a model or defiant student, you're in a position to make a difference as a student leader. One of the best ways to show appreciation for the adults who are working hard to see you succeed is by making sure you go to school, be respectful, and focus on gaining knowledge every single day in order to pave the way for the generation that will come after you.

After your family and health, education is the most important thing in your life. It is the key that opens every known door to mankind. It will set you up for success in anything you can think of, from school to sports to family to career, and the list goes on. As a matter of fact, all the individuals I mentioned earlier who are working hard to help you earn an education, would not be in a position to do so if they did not have some level of schooling and learning. A world of opportunities is waiting for you, but you cannot have access to it unless you get a good education.

When I was a teenager, I thought I knew it all. Maybe that's something you can relate to. At times, I really believed I was invincible. In reality, I was young and dumb. Although I was blessed with intellect and athletic abilities, I was deficient in maturity. About a month away from high school graduation, my counselor asked me what I planned on choosing as a major in college. I boastfully replied that it didn't matter because I was on my way to the NFL. I went as far as telling her to choose my major as a backup plan as long as it made a lot of money.

She eventually talked some sense into me, looked at my grades from middle to high school, noticed my strength in math, and suggested engineering. I said okay. I went to school and earned two degrees in engineering. When my football dream didn't work out, I started working as an engineer. I quickly realized I didn't like the profession and ended up not using those degrees. However, they gave me opportunities for me to learn skills, work at companies, and eventually become an educator. Without a college education, those doors would have been shut.

From the day you were born, your guardians, family, and educational professionals have been supporting and guiding you along your academic journey. Your victory is their satisfaction; their legacy is your destination. Can you imagine where you would be if these individuals didn't feed you, clothe you, teach you the alphabet, help you understand difficult concepts, provide feedback on your work, and encourage you to reach your full potential? Not only can I imagine it, I've seen the devastating results. I've had countless friends and classmates who didn't appreciate the love, sweat, and tears of the people in their village; they ended up either with a life of destruction or full of pain. My advice to you is: don't be that kid.

The average American teenager spends an average of 7.5 hours per day on electronics for entertainment, which equates to about 114 days for the year. This does not include the screen time for school-related activities and research. While technology is a powerful and necessary tool for today's society, you should balance your screen time with other activities. If you don't set limits on the use of technology, it will negatively impact your health and well-being.

Too much screen time can destroy your life in multiple ways. It can lead to poor sleep patterns. It has been proven that the exposure to the blue light emitted by screens can interfere with the production of the hormone melatonin that is essential for regulating sleep. As a result, this can lead to insomnia and sleep disturbances. Additionally, staring at screens for extended periods can cause eye strain, headaches, and dry eyes. These symptoms can be uncomfortable and distracting and over time lead to more serious eye problems. More often than not, you'll find yourself becoming addicted to technology or the content you're watching. Instead of resting at night, you'll find yourself sacrificing sleep to be on your device. When it's time for you to show up for class the next day, you'll be unable to be alert and stay awake. You are not in the best physical state to learn, which can eventually bleed into your mental stability. Some studies have linked excessive screen time to behavioral issues such as aggression, impulsivity, and poor self-regulation. I know this has to sound familiar to you at this point because either you or your peers have fallen victim to these effects.

The most destructive impact of screen time is obesity because it leads to a sedentary lifestyle that reduces physical activity and energy expenditure. This contributes to weight gain because you tend to eat an increased number of unhealthy snacks and beverages. Obesity is a major risk factor to cardiovascular disease, which is the leading cause of death worldwide. It has also been linked to several types of cancer, respiratory problems, and liver diseases. You might be wondering, "Why are you telling me all of this?" I'm glad you asked. It's educational! What you don't know is bigger than you, if you don't learn it, it will destroy you. It's crucial for you to understand that today's actions determine tomorrow's future. The decisions you make and the habits you follow will either hurt or help your future. The only person who can control those things is YOU.

One of the best ways to own your future is by setting goals. You need to set realistic and achievable goals, both short-term and long-term. This can help you stay focused, motivated, and have a sense of accomplishment each day. Before I offer some strategies that can help you with this journey, it's important for you to understand that different steps may work for different individuals, and a personalized approach may be necessary. At the end of the day, you have to be disciplined and consistent in order to see results. One of the most common strategies and acronyms people use for goal setting is SMART goals. It stands for Specific, Measurable, Achievable, Relevant, and Time-bound.

Specific—Goals should be specific and well-defined. Whatever it is you decide to do, you should ask yourself who, what, when, where, why, and how questions. Write your answers down on paper, so you can identify and determine clear goals.

Measurable—You should track and evaluate your progress. In other words, every week or so you should check to see whether or not you're improving. You should also be willing to make adjustments in order to reach your destination. I encourage you to find a trusted adult to help you check on your progress.

Achievable—Be realistic and set goals that you can achieve. Think about your skill set, resources, and constraints. Do some research on the thing you'd like to do to find out if it's doable for you. Find a mentor. Seek a person who's already doing what you wish to do one day, and ask them how he or she got there.

After I graduated college, a high school student asked me to help him train for football in order to fulfill his dream of earning a Division I scholarship. I helped train him, but with little experience as a starter on his team and slow foot speed, I was real with him by stating that he didn't have the physical ability and necessary experience to entice the colleges he was going after and that his best shot might be a Division II or III program. It might not have been what he wanted to hear, but it was the truth. He ended up going to college and focused on something totally different than football.

Relevant—Goals should be relevant to your interests, values, and long-term plans. It's best to take calculated steps when making choices. Don't get in the habit of doing things for the sake of doing them, or because someone else is doing it. Just like everyone is born with a unique fingerprint, you were put on this Earth to achieve greatness in something. There is at least one thing that may come naturally to you. Maybe you enjoy doing something all day, every day, whether you're getting paid for it or not. Once you identify that thing, that's the area you should spend your energy and focus on. Earlier, I mentioned how I earned two engineering degrees that I haven't used professionally. As a teenager, if I would've taken the time to explore my gifts and talents, I would've majored in creative writing or performing arts in college. Again, I'm encouraging you to find a mentor, shadow a professional, or participate in an internship. You should start doing those things as early as middle school.

Time-bound—Once you have a specific goal that's achievable and relevant for you, it's extremely important to set a specific deadline or timeline. This will provide a sense of urgency and focus. If not, it'll end up being a dream instead of reality. You'll find yourself saying you'll do it one of these days, which really means none of these days. Break down large or long-term goals into smaller, more manageable steps. This can help you avoid feeling overwhelmed. It will also give you room to celebrate your milestones and increase your sense of accomplishment as you achieve each step. For instance, if you'd like to be a scientist one day, you can challenge yourself to earn no lower than a 90-percent average in your science class and visit a science museum each quarter. That's a short-term goal that will help you learn more about the field and train yourself in the stages that will lead to your long-term goal.

When I was a classroom teacher, I did my best to challenge my students to set goals every year. One particular year, I had them designate a composition notebook for each subject and write their goals for it on the first page. At the time, I was teaching writing. Every class period came in whining about how much they hated writing and didn't want to be in my class. After we got past the complaints, they were set to attempt to reach the standards I set for them. Each quarter, they wrote the grade they wanted to earn and one area of weakness they aspired to improve. Initially, some wrote down that they wanted to pass my class. That wasn't specific enough. They revised it to document a specific percentage. I made them take it a step further by writing the goal on a piece of paper and taping it on their bathroom mirrors so they can see it every morning.

Additionally, they wrote down the challenge to practice and study notes for at least fifteen minutes a day. At the end of each week, I sat down with each of them to go over their growth and class averages to determine whether or not they were on track to meet the goals they set for themselves for the end of the quarter. There were students who did not meet their percentage goals for a semester, but we were able to celebrate the fact that their grammar improved. We compared the difference between the run-on sentences they wrote at the beginning of the year to the clarity and complexity of later sentences. Adjustments were also made to help them do better in reaching the goal the following semester.

I knew many of them wouldn't grow up to be writers, but I took the time to make writing relevant to some of the things I knew they enjoyed. Since entertainment is a huge component of the culture, I taught them that many rap and hip-hop artists don't write their own songs. Instead, they use ghostwriters. I exposed them to the world of playwriting and scriptwriting. They were amazed at how writing intersected into so many professions. That particular year, not only did their academic writing improve, but they became more disciplined, complained less about classwork, scored high on the state writing tests, and learned about a variety of writing careers they were not aware of.

Once you set academic and personal goals for yourself, they will help you stay motivated and focused on your education. I need you to believe that you have the ability to learn and grow. Your abilities can be developed through hard work and dedication. This will help you overcome challenges and setbacks. Trust me, you will fail sometimes, and that's okay. As long as you learn your lesson and do better next time. Additionally, you have to manage your time effectively. Everything is not a priority. After your health, time is the most powerful tool you have, so use it wisely. If someone or something is not helping reach your goal, then it's an automatic distraction. Once your time is wasted, it can't be recycled, and you can't get it back. It is crucial for you to know that your main priority in school is your academic responsibilities. This includes scheduling study time, avoiding procrastination, and staying on track with your coursework.

Communication is another key to your success. In order to remain on track, you must communicate with your teachers. Do not be afraid to ask questions when you don't understand something. Your educators are there to clarify your understanding of the course material and give you feedback on your progress. I can't tell you how many times I've heard students complain about how they don't like their teachers. I hear you and respect your point of view, but it shouldn't stop you from reaching your goals. I've sat in classes of many teachers I didn't necessarily care for. If I chose to allow that to keep me from doing my work, I wouldn't be where I am today.

I'll let you in on a little secret. I guarantee you that some of the adults who are working at your school do not like each other, but they have to show up to do their jobs. The same goes for your parents or guardians. Collaboration and working with people do not depend on whether you like them. It boils down to keeping your eyes on the goal that needs to be attained. You shouldn't let anyone get in the way of securing a successful future for yourself—not you, not your classmates, not your teachers, no one! You should seek to build respectful, positive, and healthy relationships with all your educators. If that doesn't happen, your job is to be respectful, get your work done, and keep it moving. Focus on the fact that the educator has valuable information you need to learn in order to advance to the next stage of your life. Lastly, the ability to coexist with others who are different from you is a life skill that will help you grow into adulthood and beyond.

There are other ways you should take responsibility for your learning. You must actively participate in class discussions and complete assignments on time. If you have classmates who are making it difficult for the teacher to teach or keeping you from staying focused, I need you to have the courage to not get involved with the disruptive behavior. This includes not laughing at them, because the minute you do that, you're giving them the attention they're seeking, which will encourage them to continue.

Additionally, being the leader that you are, you should take the responsibility to be resourceful when needed. For example, if you're working on a project, go the extra mile by asking other adults or using online apps and resources like Coursera, edX, and Khan Academy. Read widely by indulging in a variety of books and articles. If you're struggling with a subject, get together with other scholars to create a study group as a form of support or find one online through forums. I have a list of nine websites in the back of the book that can help you with being resourceful.

Lastly, I would encourage you to get involved with extracurricular activities that are aligned with your interests and passions. You'll be afforded opportunities to learn new skills and abilities outside the classroom. They can range from sports to music to volunteering. Additionally, you'll be able to build social connections with peers who share similar interests, and be of service to your community. This is the best way to foster meaningful friendships that have a sense of belonging. Trust me, following random people on social media will most likely lead you nowhere. Believe it or not, extracurricular activities can help you academically in school because they can assist with motivation, time management, and other skills.

More importantly, you'll put yourself in a position to develop leadership qualities. Activities like student government, sports teams, debate teams, and others. Ultimately, you will enhance your chances of being accepted into colleges and universities, because they often look for applicants who have demonstrated a commitment to extracurricular activities. Your participation in those things exemplify leadership, teamwork, and a willingness to take on challenges. Overall, these things will help you learn, grow, and develop important life skills that will make you more marketable and successful in the future.

Education is the one thing in your life that never gets old and should continue to grow. It starts at home. It begins with respecting your parents and authority figures, understanding your values, and honoring the people in your life who are dedicated to helping you succeed. Utilize your village—the people in your life who are serving as champions to support you. Ask and seek help. Everyone has had assistance at some point in life.

Lastly, love yourself enough to recognize that you are in the driver's seat of your education, and that you shouldn't allow anyone or anything to keep you from getting to your destination. Think of education as a smartphone with a password that has access to all the apps and unlimited resources you need in life. Every educator who teaches you each year has a piece of the password you need to unlock the possibilities that await you. Although learning new things can be challenging, your hard work and dedication will be enough to help you overcome your struggles. When you fail, embrace the lessons and try again as a stronger individual. When you accomplish a goal or grow, take pride in your achievement by celebrating the wins, whether big or small. You are born to add value to the world. We're waiting for your greatness. No one can do what you were born to do in the way it was meant to be done, until you do it.

## CHAPTER TAKEAWAYS

There are people around YOU who are working hard to make sure YOU succeed. None of their efforts matter if YOU don't work hard to make sure success happens.

- The decisions you make and the habits you follow will either hurt or help your future.
- You were created on this Earth to achieve greatness in something.
- Once your time is wasted, it can't be recycled, and you can't get it back.
- You shouldn't let anyone get in the way of securing a successful future for yourself—not you, not your classmates, not your teachers, no one!
- Education is the one thing in your life that never gets old and should continue to grow.

## PROBE AND TRANSFORM

In your opinion, why is education important for personal growth and development? How does it help individuals explore their interests, discover their talents, and reach their full potential?

- What are some ways in which education can empower individuals and communities?
- Can you think of any examples where lack of education has hindered individuals or communities?
- How can you use your education to make a positive impact on others and contribute to the betterment of society?

# CONCLUSION

A s the final notes echo through the pages of this book, a resounding sense of peace flows within my heart. I've always wanted to create a platform to reach educational stakeholders so that we all might work cohesively. In this profound symphony, we have encountered the unwavering dedication of guardians, the visionary leadership of principals, the transformative influence of teachers, the community's embrace of collective progress, and the boundless potential of students. Through their interconnectedness, we have discovered that the true essence of education lies not in isolation but in collaboration, not in individual efforts but in the harmonious symphony of stakeholders united by a shared vision.

For it is through their tireless advocacy, and their boundless belief in the potential of every learner, that the orchestra of education reaches its crescendo, resonating with the promise of a brighter future. As we bid farewell to these pages, let this book be a beacon, igniting the flames of empowerment and nurturing the seeds of change within the hearts and minds of all who bear witness to its timeless wisdom.

This book has shed light on the critical issue of accountability in fostering respect and growth within the field of education. While the shared commitment towards educational excellence may seem daunting, it's attainable if everyone is in the constant state of learning and growing. Collectively, we will work towards creating a positive and thriving educational environment. Trust me, the change won't happen overnight, so don't grow weary, and keep doing your best. Be sure to leverage your go-to person, or people, who can hold you up when you're feeling down. Through it all, I want you to keep these nuggets in mind:

- Parents must actively engage in their child's education, fostering a respectful and supportive home environment. They should communicate regularly with teachers, attend parent–teacher meetings, and advocate for their child's needs. Encouraging a culture of respect at home can greatly influence a student's attitude towards learning and growth.

- Policymakers have the power to shape the educational landscape. They should prioritize policies that promote respect and growth, such as fostering inclusive and diverse learning environments, providing equitable access to resources and opportunities, and supporting professional development for educators. By aligning policy decisions with the values of respect and growth, they can drive positive change throughout the education system.

- Principals play a pivotal role in setting the tone for their schools. They should create a respectful and nurturing school culture where all stakeholders are valued and supported. This can be achieved by promoting open communication, establishing clear expectations, and fostering professional development opportunities for teachers. Principals should also implement strategies to encourage a growth mindset among students, allowing them to embrace challenges and learn from their mistakes.

- Teachers have a direct impact on students' growth and development. They should foster a classroom environment that promotes respect, empathy, and growth. Teachers should implement innovative teaching methods, personalized instruction, and ongoing assessment practices to cater to individual student needs. Additionally, they should provide timely and constructive feedback to facilitate student growth and instill a love for learning.

- Community leaders should collaborate with educational institutions to create strong partnerships that foster respect and growth. They can support initiatives that promote community involvement in schools, such as mentoring programs, internships, and workshops. By valuing and investing in education, community leaders can contribute to a culture of respect and growth that extends beyond the classroom walls.
- Students themselves have a responsibility to cultivate respect and foster their own growth. They should actively engage in their learning journey, demonstrate respect for their peers and teachers, and embrace opportunities for personal and academic growth. By adopting a growth mindset, students can develop resilience, overcome challenges, and continuously strive for improvement.

By embracing accountability and focusing on respect and growth, these stakeholders can collectively transform the field of education. Through collaborative efforts, ongoing communication, and a commitment to continuous improvement, we can create an educational ecosystem that celebrates diversity, fosters respect, and empowers individuals to reach their full potential. Ultimately, this will lead to a brighter and more promising future for generations to come.

# REFERENCES

American Association of University Women (AAUW) Report: "Why So Few? Women in Science, Technology, Engineering, and Mathematics" (2010) - This report explores the gender biases and stereotypes that contribute to the underrepresentation of women in STEM fields, including biases starting from early education. [Source: American Association of University Women, "Why So Few? Women in Science, Technology, Engineering, and Mathematics"]

American School & University magazine (2019) retrieved from https://www.asumag.com/

Anakwe, U. P., & Greenhaus, J. H. (2000). "Prior work experience and social-ization experiences of college graduates." International Journal of Manpower, 21(2), 95-111.

Arnold, K. D., Soto, E. B., Wartman, K. L., Methven, L., & Brown, P. G. (2015). "Post-secondary outcomes of innovative high schools: The big picture longitudinal study." Submitted for consideration for publication in Teachers College Record. Retrieved from: https://1.cdn.edl.io/9hloszW4FyNM5Ed-JWri39BVKbVpArurU9gAFe3FmKmcuICyK.pdf

Barron, B., & Darling-Hammond, L. (2008). "Teaching for meaningful learning: A review of research on inquiry-based and cooperative learning." In L. Darling-Hammond, B. Barron, P.D. Pearson, A.H. Schoenfeld, E.K. Stage, T.D. Zimmerman, G.N. Cervetti, & J.L. Tilson,

Bhaskaran K, Douglas I, Forbes H, dos-Santos-Silva I, Leon DA, Smeeth L. Body-mass index and risk of 22 specific cancers: a population-based cohort study of 5.24 million UK adults. The Lancet. 2014;384(9945):755-765. doi:10.1016/S0140-6736(14)60892-8

Biddle SJH, Garcia Bengoechea E, Pedisic Z, Bennie J, Vergeer I, Wiesner G. Screen Time, Other Sedentary Behaviours, and Obesity Risk in Adults: A Review of Reviews. Curr Obes Rep. 2017;6(2):134-147. doi:10.1007/s13679-017-0256-2

Centers for Disease Control and Prevention, "Health Effects of Lead Exposure," https://www.cdc.gov/nceh/lead/prevention/health-effects.htm.

Collaboration NCDRF. Worldwide trends in body-mass index, underweight, overweight, and obesity from 1975 to 2016: a pooled analysis of 2416 population-based measurement studies in 128·9 million children, adolescents, and adults. The Lancet. 2017;390(10113):2627-2642. doi:10.1016/S0140-6736(17)32129-3

Darling-Hammond, Linda. (2009). Teacher Education and the American Future. Journal of Teacher Education. Volume 61, Issue 1-2_https://doi.org/10.1177/00224871093480

Dweck CS. Mindset: The new psychology of success. Random House; 2008.

Education Systems Center at NIU & Jobs for the Future. (2019). "Recommended technical and essential employability competencies for college and career pathway endorsements." Retrieved from: https://www.jff.org/resources/postsecondary-workforce-readiness-act/.

Fancsali, C., Jaffe-Walter, R., & Dessein, L. (2013). Student agency practices in the middle shift learning networks. Raikes Foundation.

Ferguson, D. L., & Mueller, M. K. (2017). Beyond school walls: A review of the literature on community resources that facilitate student success. Journal of Education for Students Placed at Risk, 22(1-2), 1-17.

Galassi, J. P., Gulledge, S. A., & Cox, N. D. (1997). "Planning and maintaining sound advisory programs." Middle School Journal, 28(5), 35-41.

Gonzalez-DeHass, A. R., & Willems, P. P. (2003). Examining the relationship between parental involvement and student motivation. Educational Psychology Review, 15(2), 1-22.

Grayson, J. L., & Alvarez, H. K. (2008). School leadership influences: A framework for examining leadership at the school, teacher, and student levels. Journal of School Leadership, 18(5), 490-520.

Greater Good in Education "Kindness and Compassion for Students" retrieved from https://ggie.berkeley.edu/student-well-being/kindness-and-compassion-for-students/#tab   2

Hagenauer, G. and Volet, S.E. (2014) Teacher-Student Relationship at University: An Important Yet Under-Researched Field. Oxford Review of Education, 40, 370-388. https://doi.org/10.1080/03054985.2014.921613

Hammond, Z. (2015). Culturally responsive teaching and the brain. Thousand Oaks, CA: Corwin.

Harvard Family Research Project (2006)
"Family Involvement Makes a Difference in School Success"
Retrieved from https://archive.globalfrp.org/family-involvement/publications-resources/family-involvement-makes-a-difference-in-school-success

Hattie, J. (2009). Visible learning: A synthesis of over 800 meta-analyses relating to achievement. London, UK: Routledge.

Larmer, J. & Mergendoller, J.R. (2014). "8 essentials for project-based learning." Buck Institute for Education.

Levine, E. (2010). "The rigors and rewards of internships." Educational Leadership, 68(1), 44-48.

Maehr ML, Meyer HA. Understanding Motivation and Schooling: Where We've Been, Where We Are, and Where We Need to Go. Educational Psychology Review. 2019;31(4):675-694. doi:10.1007/s10648-019-09478-1

Karoly P, Kilburn MR, Cannon JS. Early Childhood Interventions: Proven Results, Future Promise. RAND Corporation; 2005. https://www.rand.org/pubs/research_briefs/RB9143.html.

Klassen RM, Klassen JR. Self-regulation strategies in post-secondary students: a review of the literature. Canadian Journal of School Psychology. 2018;33(3):268-289. doi:10.1177/0829573518799357

Lillard, A. S., Lerner, M. D., Hopkins, E. J., Dore, R. A., Smith, E. D., & Palmquist, C. M. (2013). The impact of pretend play on children's development: A review of the evidence. American Journal of Play, 6(1), 52-72.

Maertz Jr, C. P., Stoeberl, P. A., & Marks, J. (2014). "Building successful internships: Lessons from the research for interns, schools, and employers." Career Development International, 19(1), 123-142.

National Academies of Sciences, Engineering, and Medicine. (2018). How people learn II: Learners, contexts, and cultures. Washington, DC: The National Academies Press.

National Center for Education Statistics (NCES) Report: "The Condition of Education 2020" - This report provides data on racial disparities in access to advanced courses and resources, indicating persistent inequities in educational opportunities. [Source: National Center for Education Statistics, "The Condition of Education 2020"]

National Center for Family Literacy. (2008). Early Childhood Education: The Importance of Family Involvement. Retrieved from https://www.familieslearning.org/wp-content/uploads/2017/05/ECE_The_Importance_of_Family_Involvement.pdf

National Education Association (NEA) Research: NEA's research on ELL students highlights the challenges they face in receiving appropriate language support, culturally responsive instruction, and inclusive educational experiences. [Source: National Education Association, "Ensuring Culturally Responsive Instruction for ELLs"]

Oakes, J. (2008). "Keeping track: Structuring equality and inequality in an era of accountability." The Teachers College Record, 110(3), 700-712.

Parents Are Teachers Too https://www.schoolfamily.com/school-family-articles/article/823-parents-are-teachers-too

Piché M-È, Poirier P, Lemieux I, Després J-P. Overview of Epidemiology and Contribution of Obesity and Body Fat Distribution to Cardiovascular Disease: An Update. Progress in Cardiovascular Diseases. 2018;61(2):103-113. doi:10.1016/j.pcad.2018.06.004

Pintrich PR. A motivational science perspective on the role of student motivation in learning and teaching contexts. Journal of Educational Psychology. 2003;95(4):667-686. doi:10.1037/0022-0663.95.4.667

Pintrich PR, De Groot EV. Motivational and self-regulated learning components of classroom academic performance. Journal of Educational Psychology. 1990;82(1):33-40. doi:10.1037//0022-0663.82.1.33

Rich, Dorothy (2008). "Megaskills-Building Our Children's Character and Achievement for School and Life." Sourcebooks

Rossmann, M. (2015). Involving children in household tasks: Is it worth the effort? The University of Minnesota Publication.

Rubin, B. C., & Noguera, P. A. (2004). "Tracking detracking: Sorting through the dilemmas and possibilities of detracking in practice." Equity & Excellence in Education, 37(1), 92-101.

Rui, N. (2009). "Four decades of research on the effects of detracking reform: Where do we stand?—A systematic review of the evidence."

Shriberg, David. (2020) The Present and Future of Consultation: The importance of Developing and Nurturing Family-Professional Partnerships. *Journal of Educational and Psychological Consultation* 30:4, pages 395-401.

Sideridis GD, Kaplan A. Goal setting, academic self-concept, and the moderating role of self-efficacy among adolescents. European Journal of Psychology of Education. 2010;25(4):473-489. doi:10.1007/s10212-010-0029-8

Smitka K, Perales-Puchalt J, Rodríguez-Martín B, Pérez-Cruzado D. The Association between Screen Time and Obesity: A Review of Current Evidence. Nutrients. 2020;12(12):3795. doi:10.3390/nu12123795

Steinberg, A. (1998). Real learning, real work: School-to-work as high school reform. New York, NY: Routledge.

The Aspen Institute. (2018). "From a nation at risk to a nation at hope: Recommendations from the National Commission on Social, Emotional, & Academic Development." Retrieved from: https://search.issuelab.org/resource/from-a-nation-at-risk-to-a-nation-at-hope-recommendations-from-the-national-commission-on-social-emotional-academic-development.html

The Center for Parenting Education. Part I Benefits of Chores https://centerforparentingeducation.org/library-of-articles/responsibility-and-chores/part-i-benefits-of-chores/#:~:text=The%20Research&text=Research%20indicates%20that%20those%20children,to%20greater%20success%20in%20school

The Education Trust Report: "Funding Gaps 2018" - This report highlights the inequitable distribution of funding between schools serving low-income students and those serving affluent students, leading to resource disparities and educational inequities. [Source: The Education Trust, "Funding Gaps 2018"]

"The Role of Communities in Education" by the National Center for Education Statistics: https://nces.ed.gov/pubs2004/2004313.pdf

Thomas, J. W. (2000). A review of research on project-based learning. San Rafael, CA: The Autodesk Foundation. Retrieved from: https://my.pblworks. org/resource/document/a_review_of_research_on_project_based_learning.

U.S. Department of Education Data: Data from the Office for Civil Rights (OCR) indicates disparities in the identification, placement, and discipline of students with disabilities, suggesting potential biases within the special education system. [Source: U.S. Department of Education, Office for Civil Rights, "2017-2018 Civil Rights Data Collection: A First Look"]

U.S. Government Accountability Office (GAO) Report: "Discipline Disparities for Black Students, Boys, and Students with Disabilities" (2018) - This report highlights the disparities in disciplinary actions, showing that Black students, boys, and students with disabilities are disproportionately disciplined at higher rates compared to their peers. [Source: U.S. GAO Report, GAO-18-258]

University of Houston Graduate College of Social Work. "A Conversation on Race and Privilege with Angela Davis and Jane Elliott." Youtube, uploaded by UHGCSW, 6 September 2018, https://www.youtube.com/watch?v=S0jf-8D5WHoo

Where Do Mass Shootings Take Place? https://www.bloomberg.com/news/articles/2018-03-01/all-kinds-of-u-s-communities-have-suffered-mass-shootings

Wijarnpreecha K, Thongprayoon C, Panjawatanan P, et al. Obesity and risk of nonalcoholic fatty liver disease: A systematic review and meta-analysis. Journal of Clinical Gastroenterology. 2018;52(2):140-146. doi:10.1097/MCG.0000000000000761

Yao Y, Chen Y, Wang S, et al. The relationship between screen time and childhood obesity: a systematic review and meta-analysis. Obes Res Clin Pract. 2021;15(1):1-11. doi:10.1016/j.orcp.2020.10.004

# ONLINE RESOURCES FOR STUDENTS

1. Khan Academy: https://www.khanacademy.org/
2. Coursera: https://www.coursera.org/
3. edX: https://www.edx.org/
4. Duolingo: https://www.duolingo.com/
5. Quizlet: https://quizlet.com/
6. Photomath: https://photomath.app/
7. Science fairs: https://www.societyforscience.org/isef/
8. Robotics teams: https://www.firstinspires.org/
9. Starting a blog: https://www.wpbeginner.com/start-a-wordpress-blog/

www.ingramcontent.com/pod-product-compliance
Lightning Source LLC
Chambersburg PA
CBHW050448150626
46551CB00029B/1990